Stop Reading the News

Withdrawn
from Stock

Also by Rolf Dobelli

The Art of Thinking Clearly
The Art of the Good Life

Stop Reading the News

A Manifesto for a Happier, Calmer and Wiser Life

ROLF DOBELLI

TRANSLATED BY CAROLINE WAIGHT

SCEPTRE

Originally published in Germany in 2019 by Piper
Verlag GmbH, München / Berlin
First published in Great Britain in 2020 by Sceptre
An Imprint of Hodder & Stoughton
An Hachette UK company

This paperback edition published in 2021

1

A CIP catalogue record for this title is available from the British Library

Paperback ISBN 9781529342727
eBook ISBN 9781529342697

Typeset in Sabon by Hewer Text UK Ltd, Edinburgh
Printed and bound in Great Britain by Clays Ltd, Elcograf S.p.A.

Hodder & Stoughton policy is to use papers that are natural, renewable
and recyclable products and made from wood grown in sustainable
forests. The logging and manufacturing processes are expected to
conform to the environmental regulations of the country of origin.

Hodder & Stoughton Ltd
Carmelite House
50 Victoria Embankment
London EC4Y 0DZ

www.sceptrebooks.co.uk

To my wife, Sabine, who stopped reading the news long before I did. And to our twins, Numa and Avi, who thankfully are still too young for all that.

CONTENTS

Stop Reading the News

YOU COULD HAVE
HEARD A PIN DROP

On 12 April 2013 I was invited by the *Guardian* to talk about my book *The Art of Thinking Clearly*, which had just been published in English. Each week an author is given the opportunity to briefly present his or her latest book to the editorial staff, and that week the honour was mine. Then editor-in-chief Alan Rusbridger gathered his staff. The room slowly filled with journalists, until roughly fifty of them were standing in front of me with their morning coffee in their hands, murmuring and waiting for Rusbridger to introduce me. My wife had come with me, and I was squeezing her hand as I tried to keep my nerves in check. These were the brightest minds at one of the world's most prominent newspapers, and I had been given the unique privilege of sharing with them a few of my aperçus from the world of cognitive science in the hope that one of them would write about my book. After clearing his throat, Rusbridger got to his feet and said dryly, 'I was just on your website and noticed your new article. I'd like you to speak about that, *not* about your new book.'

I wasn't prepared for this. On the tip of my tongue were various practised, hopefully convincing, well-formulated observations on *The Art of Thinking Clearly*, which ideally would find their way unaltered into the pages of the *Guardian*. I swallowed them. The article Rusbridger had found on my website listed the most important arguments against consuming precisely what these internationally respected professionals spent their days producing: the news. Throwing caution to the wind, I began to talk, serving up reason after reason for why it's best to avoid the news. Now, instead of standing in front of fifty people well disposed to me, I was confronted by fifty opponents. Caught in the crossfire of their stares, I tried to stay as calm as possible. After twenty minutes I'd reached the end of my argument, concluding with the words, 'Let's be honest: what you're doing here, ladies and gentlemen, is basically entertainment.'

Silence. You could have heard a pin drop. Rusbridger narrowed his eyes, glanced around and said, 'I'd like us to publish Mr Dobelli's arguments. Today.' He turned around and left the room without saying goodbye. The journalists followed him. Nobody looked at me. Nobody said so much as a word.

Four hours later there was an abridged version of my article on the *Guardian* website. Before long it had accrued 450 comments from readers – the maximum the website would allow. My piece, 'News is bad for you', was para-doxically one of the most-read newspaper articles of the year.

The book you hold in your hands is based on this contro-versial article. But it contains far more: more reasons not to consume the news, more research on the impact of reading the news, and more tips on how we can kick the habit. Digitalisation has turned the news from a harmless form of entertainment into a weapon of mass destruction, and it's aimed straight at our mental health. We need to get out of the way.

One thing is crucial to note here: restricting your consumption of the news doesn't have to be a sacrifice. You'll be richly rewarded – with more time and fresh eyes for what truly matters, what truly makes you happy.

A few weeks after this book first came out, the COVID-19 tsunami washed over the globe. One Dutch journalist wrote: 'Shouldn't we call Dobelli and let him know?' I am no hermit, so of course the pandemic didn't escape me. After sampling a few online articles to see what the panic was all about, I quickly went back to my News Diet that has served me so well for so long.

On a TV interview a little later, a journalist asked: 'How are you keeping up with the pandemic and important corona related restrictions?' My answer was: the same way journalists keep up with it, by looking what the experts and the government say. There are plenty of good university lectures and research papers online to understand the virus and the epidemiology. And to keep myself abreast of fresh restrictions: every country has an official website that spells out what current measures are in effect. In a nutshell, I go straight to the source. No detour through the news swamp. It was obvious to me: with regards to COVID-19 journalists don't enjoy superior knowledge. Just as they

3

don't for every other subject they might report on, too. To keep a calm head about the world, abstain from the news and go directly to the source. It has never been easier. And it has never been more important or made more sense.

1

HOW I GAVE UP THE NEWS: PART 1

'Hello, my name is Rolf, and I'm a news-aholic.' If there were self-help groups for news junkies like there are for alcoholics, that's how I would have introduced myself to the group, hoping they would understand. That was more than ten years ago.

It all started so normally. Born into a middle-class family, I grew up with the usual news routine. If you, too, were young in the seventies, you'll probably recognise it. Every weekday at half past six in the morning I listened as the paperboy dropped the newspaper into the letterbox by the front door. Moments later my mother opened the door a crack and snatched the paper out of the box with a practised flick of the wrist – she didn't even have to step outside. On her way into the kitchen she divided the paper into two sections, placing one in front of my father (she decided which one) and keeping the other for herself. While we enjoyed our breakfast, my parents leafed through their respective sections, then swapped. At seven o'clock on the dot, we listened to the news bulletin on the Swiss national radio station DRS. Not long after that, my father set off for work and we children were dispatched to school. At noon the whole family gathered around the table for lunch. Afterwards, around 12.30 p.m., it was time for more radio news. Ditto at dinnertime, around 6.30. At half past seven came the highlight of the evening: *Tagesschau*, a current affairs programme on Swiss National TV (the BBC of Switzerland).

The news was as much a part of my life as Ovaltine at breakfast. Yet, even then, I had the vague feeling that something wasn't right. It baffled me that the newspaper arrived in the same thickness and format every single day. The local paper, to which my parents subscribed, *Luzerner Neuste Nachrichten*, consisted of a one-page foreign affairs section, a one-page financial section, a two-page section on the city of Lucerne and so on. It didn't matter how much or how little had happened the day before. In those days there were no Sunday papers in Switzerland, but the Monday edition was the same length (thirty-six pages) as the others, even though it covered two days – Saturday *and* Sunday. I thought that was odd. If something happened on an uneventful day it would be treated as important and given centre stage, even if on a busy day it would have been treated as unimportant. 'I guess that's just the way it is,' I thought – and put it out of my mind.

As the years passed I turned into a voracious newspaper reader. At the age of seventeen this hunger for news from across the world reached its first apex. I would read any newspaper I could get my hands on from cover to cover, omitting only the sports section. As my friends whiled away their time in the woods, on the football pitch, with model aeroplanes or with girls, I spent whole Saturdays in the reading room at the library in Lucerne. The newspapers were clamped into a wooden stick so that you could hang them up on a peg and the pages wouldn't fall out. Most of them were so big and the sticks so long and heavy that my wrist would start aching if I sat in one of the armchairs and tried to hold them, so instead I'd settle at one of the enormous desks and read it like a priest turning the pages of a Bible on the altar. I'd even have to keep standing up and leaning across the table to read the articles printed at the very top.

Every day at the same hour I'd see the same elderly gentlemen in horn-rimmed glasses and suits and ties – in arch-conservative Lucerne, people still dressed that way on the weekend – avidly reading the newspapers. These gentlemen struck me as infinitely clever, and I hoped one day I'd look as wise and well-read as them. And when I read the newspapers, that's exactly how I felt. I fancied myself an informed young man, unimpressed by the banalities of everyday life – a high-flying intellectual. Presidents shaking hands, natural disasters, attempted coups: this was the wide world, the world that really mattered – and I felt a part of it.

When I started university my obsession with the news got pushed into the background; as a student I simply had too many books to read. But as soon as I started my first job, the news-reading urge returned with a vengeance. As financial controller for Swissair, I spent nearly every day on a plane. When the flight attendant came round with a stack of newspapers, I'd grab the lot. If I couldn't 'process' all of them during the flight, I'd stuff the ones I hadn't read into my briefcase (an angular thing with a combination lock on either side of the handle, the kind you only see these days in low-budget crime dramas, used to transport bundles of dollar bills) and finish them later in my hotel room. Reading all these international newspapers and magazines gave me a sense of near euphoria. It felt like I was shining a light on every single facet of the world every single day. I was ecstatic.

2

HOW I GAVE UP THE NEWS: PART 2

I hadn't just fallen for newspapers, magazines, TV and radio. With the advent of the internet in the 1990s, suddenly there was even more to know. Suddenly there was *everything*. News poured in from every corner of the earth, comprehensive, immediate and free. I remember my first screensaver. Rather than displaying some boring bouncing triangle, it showed the latest headlines. It was called PointCast, and I could spend hours sitting in front of it: the headlines scrolled non-stop like in Times Square, but on my very own screen! Meanwhile the major newspapers and magazines were busy setting up their own websites, and many local papers followed suit. By now you were never really finished reading the news; you couldn't be, there was always another headline to read, and by the time you had exhausted those ones, the others already had new headlines and new news.

The second and third generations of internet browsers enabled push notifications and RSS feeds. I subscribed to the lot. The newspapers offered daily newsletters. I signed up to those, too. News podcasts appeared. Couldn't let myself miss those, could I? It felt like I had my finger on the pulse. I was ardent, intoxicated, drunk. It was like alcohol. Only, I thought, it didn't dull your mind – it sharpened it.

In fact, the news is every bit as dangerous as alcohol. Even more so, actually, because the obstacles to boozing are much harder to overcome. Or, to put it more accurately, there *are* obstacles to drinking, whereas you are actively encouraged to read the news. It takes effort to buy alcohol. Time, money. Alcohol will not be delivered free to your home. If you do become an alcoholic and you're (still) in a relationship, you may have to get creative in hiding the bottles from your partner and getting rid of them when they're empty. Frankly, it's a hassle. The news, however, is not. The news is everywhere, the majority of it is free, and it sidles automatically into your brain. You don't have to store it anywhere, and there's nothing to dispose of afterwards. These 'negative obstacles' are what make the news so insidious. I didn't realise this until much later, by which time I'd spent tens of thousands of hours consuming the news. I asked myself two questions: do you understand the world better now? And: do you make better decisions? The answer in both cases was no.

Yet I still felt inexorably drawn to the overwhelming, garish parade of news, even though it was clearly making me anxious. Fragments of news reports were constantly intruding into my reality, and I was suddenly finding it difficult to read longer texts in one go. It was as though somebody had carved up my attention into tiny pieces. I started to panic that I'd never be able to recover my attention span, that I'd never again be able to assemble these fragments into a whole. Slowly, I began to detach myself from the theatre of news. I deleted the newsletters and the RSS feeds and tried to restrict myself to only a few websites. Yet even that was too much. So I scaled it down further – five sources, then four, then three, then two – and allowed myself only three visits to news sites per day. That didn't work either. I swung from link to link like an orangutan, rapidly getting lost in the endless jungle of news. I needed a radical solution, and I needed it *now*. And so one day I decided: no more news. Full stop. The decision was drastic and immediate, and it worked.

Liberating myself from a news addiction took time, willpower and a readiness to experiment. Above all, I was seeking answers to the following questions: what is the news? What makes it so irresistible? What happens in our brains when we consume it? How can we be so well informed yet know so little?

Renouncing the news in such a drastic manner was particularly tough because many of my friends are journalists. They are some of the most intelligent, funny and sophisticated people I know. Moreover, they chose their profession mainly on moral grounds – to make the world a little bit better and hold those in power to account. Unfortunately, they are now trapped in an industry that has virtually nothing to do with real journalism. All this juggling of the news has made it meaningless.

Today, I'm 'clean'. Since 2010 I've been entirely news-free, and I can see, feel and report first-hand the effects of this freedom: improved quality of life, clearer thinking, more valuable insights, and vastly more time. I've cancelled my newspaper subscriptions, stopped watching TV news,

11

tuned out of the radio bulletins and stopped exposing myself to online news. It started out as a personal experiment, but now it's a philosophy of life. When I ask you to give up the news, I can do so with a clear conscience. It will make your life better. And trust me: you're not missing anything important.

NEWS IS TO THE MIND WHAT SUGAR IS TO THE BODY

What exactly is the news? This is the most basic definition: 'information on events from across the world'. A bus accident in Australia. An earthquake in Guatemala. President A is meeting President B. Actress C has divorced celebrity D. A cabinet reshuffle in Italy. A missile launch in North Korea. A record-breaking app. A man from Texas eats five kilos of live worms. An international corporation fires its CEO. An awkward tweet from a politician. There's a new Secretary-General of the United Nations. A man stabs his grandmother. The list of candidates for the Nobel Prize. A peace agreement. A shark bites off a diver's leg. China is building a new aircraft carrier. A bribery scandal. The European Central Bank warns of a recession. Summits of the G7, G20. Argentina is bankrupt. A businessman ends up in jail. A prime minister steps down. A coup. A shipping accident. The closing price of the Dow Jones.

Sometimes the media rather grandiosely calls these snippets of information 'breaking news' or 'top world headlines'. This doesn't change the fact that they're largely irrelevant to your personal world. You can safely assume that the more 'breaking' the news, the less it actually matters to you.

In comparison to books, news is a recent invention. The format is barely 350 years old. There is no specific day when the news was invented. Shortly after the invention of the printing press, around 1450, pamphlets with a broad readership came into circulation. For the most part they consisted of opinion pieces, in today's parlance, and were often religious or political propaganda. Developing in parallel to this was a private newsletter industry, which worked on a subscription basis. These newsletters were very expensive, tailored to an elite class of merchants and bankers. They reported on everything from political upheavals to harvests, both domestically and abroad, and they listed arrival times of merchant trading ships, what cargo they carried and which port they were docking at – the kind of detailed, highly specialised information you might find in a business newsletter today. The first true newspapers, which conveyed information from around the world and were intended for a wide audience, started to be circulated in the early seventeenth century. The very first was a weekly paper in Strasbourg, the *Relation aller Fürnemmen und gedenckwürdigen Historien* (1605), then one in the Saxon town of Wolfenbüttel. Newspaper mania leapt from Germany to Amsterdam to London and finally across all of Europe. By 1640, there were nine newspapers in Amsterdam alone. The first daily newspaper appeared in 1650, the *Einkommende Zeitungen* in Leipzig. A few decades later there were hundreds of dailies across

Europe. The news had finally become a business. Anything that might pique readers' interest and boost sales was considered newsworthy by the publishers, regardless of whether it was actually important. This fundamental fraud – the new being sold as the relevant – has persisted to this day. It remains the dominant model in print, online, on social media, the radio and television.

What has intensified since these early newspapers is the audacity, the vehemence and the volume with which the new is advertised as relevant. In the past twenty years, since the advent of the internet and the smartphone, our addiction to the news has become a dangerous mania. You can barely escape it. It's high time we reconsidered our approach to this glut of news. It's high time we realised the impact of consuming it and began a detox.

But perhaps there is a way of gathering information that is not marred with the challenges we find in news consumption. Are there formats that have the power to deliver real understanding, yet are not addictive? Long-form pieces are the opposite of the news: long newspaper and magazine articles, essays, features, reportage, documentaries and books. Much of their content is valuable, providing new insights and background information. But be careful: these formats are far from a guarantee of relevance. As long as they're published in media primarily financed through advertising, there's a danger that even they will prioritise novelty value above relevance. I personally don't want to agonise whether to read a long-form article every single time something piques my interest, so I've simply instituted a blanket ban on reading anything in newspapers (print and online) as well as listening to the radio and watching the TV. It's also worth pointing out that many of these long, high-quality pieces are surrounded by vacuous nonsense that rains down on readers like cheap confetti. In other words, they're often contaminated by the news. And I don't want to drink from contaminated sources. I've chosen a radical path, I know. In the following chapters I will show how you, too, can choose to free yourself from the toxic grip of the news.

There's no question that the dross we're spoon-fed every day is not only completely worthless but actively damaging. In the past few decades we've learned to recognise the many hazards of poor nutrition: insulin resistance, obesity, susceptibility to inflammation and fatigue. All of these factors can contribute to an early death. We've altered our diets and learned to resist the siren call of sugar and other simple carbohydrates. We've now reached a similar point with the news; we think about it today much as we thought about sugar and fast food twenty years ago. News is to the mind what sugar is to the body: appetising, easily digestible and extremely damaging. The media is feeding us titbits that taste palatable but do nothing to satisfy our hunger for knowledge. Unlike books and well-researched long-form articles, the news cannot satiate us. We can gobble down as many articles as we like, but we will never be doing more than gorging on sweets. As with sugar, alcohol, fast food and smoking, the side effects only become apparent later.

A healthy diet is important for the body, but good psychological nutrition is equally crucial. Consider this book a manifesto against the all-you-can-eat menu of the daily news. So stay strong. Cold turkey is always hard. But it's worth it.

4

RADICAL ABSTINENCE

Have I just opened your eyes? If the answer's yes, then read no more. What you should do *right now* is this: banish the news from your life. Opt out. Radically. Make it as difficult as possible for you to access your usual news sources. Unsubscribe from all their newsletters. Delete the news apps on your phone and your iPad *right this minute*. Sell your TV. Delete all the news pages from the favourites in your browser. Don't choose a news site as your homepage. Instead, choose a page that never changes – the more unassuming, the better.

When you travel, always take plenty of good books. If you're on the train or an aeroplane and you notice a newspaper lying around, leave it alone. You'll gain nothing by flicking through it. Deliberately turn your gaze away from the headlines and towards something more productive. Just leave the paper or magazine where you found it – I don't care how seductively it tempts you.

Airports often place enormous stands brimming with dozens of free newspapers throughout the terminals. Walk straight on. Most of them are nothing but vapid advertising. If you're waiting at the gate, sit far away from the screens pumping news into the terminal. The talking heads on TV news are the last thing your brain needs. Ideally you want to be working, reading a book or calmly watching the world go by as you let your mind wander.

If you want to maintain the illusion of 'not missing anything important in the world', I suggest skimming a round-up section in some of the international and local media – the *Economist* has a weekly double-page feature called 'The world this week' and the *Week* is specifically geared towards summing up the week's news. Above all, read magazines and books that aren't afraid – and have the resources – to present the world in all its complexity. Newspapers and magazines that primarily feature articles by experts are also valuable. You could also give a few long-form publications a chance – there are many good examples to choose from. The world is a complicated place. Try to read a book a week. If after twenty pages it hasn't expanded or altered your world view, or otherwise managed to capture your attention, put it aside. If, on the other hand, you find a book that tells you something new on every other page, read it cover to cover. Then read it again, straight away. When you read something a second time, it's not twice as effective as the first read-through – in my experience, it's more like ten times as powerful. I'd also recommend reading long-form articles twice, too.

Now and again, it's worth reading textbooks. There is no better nourishment for the mind. A textbook is as intensive and nutritious as a bachelor's degree. You need a basis upon which to understand the world, and textbooks are especially well suited to developing one. Sounds unsexy, but it's true. The better the base of your understanding – whether that comes from textbooks or study – the easier it is to understand new ideas.

Oh, and Google is allowed! The internet is full of top-notch sources of information. Occasionally your searches will take you to a news site. This isn't a disaster. You simply have to make sure you're not sucked into the whirlpool of other articles vying for your attention. *You* have to decide what you're looking for. *You* have to set your own path. Don't let the object of your attention be dictated by the news media.

For ten years I've consistently practised what I preach. The impact on my quality of life and decision-making has been remarkable. Try it. You've got nothing to lose. You have so much to gain.

5

THE THIRTY-DAY PLAN

The first week of radical abstinence will be the worst. Not checking the news takes discipline. In the beginning you'll be on tenterhooks, expecting at any moment that something terrible will happen in the world. You'll feel itchy, nervous, unprepared for the next catastrophe. You'll think you're at a disadvantage compared to everybody else. You'll feel excluded, even socially isolated. You'll constantly be tempted to steal a glimpse at your favourite news sites. Resist. Stick to your plan. Go for thirty days without the news. Tell yourself, 'After thirty days I'll be free to return to my old life. But for those thirty days, I'll stick it out.' Why thirty days? Because by then you'll have started to experience the first waves of calm and inner peace. You'll realise you have much more time and concentration, that you better understand the world.

After thirty days you'll reach an important turning point: you'll realise that, despite abstaining from the news, you've not missed any relevant information – nor will you miss any in the future. If something truly significant happens, you'll find out soon enough – from the specialised press, from your friends, your family, or someone you're chatting to. When you meet up with friends, ask them if anything important has happened in the world. The question is an ideal conversation-starter. The usual answer? 'Not really, no.'

After thirty days you can decide whether you want to return to your old news-contaminated life. If you do, and you later change your mind, you'll have to go back to square one and survive those first difficult thirty days once more. Most people who've followed my recommendation, however, are still news-free today, because the advantages of this fresh approach to life vastly outweigh the downsides.

If the first thirty days are already behind you – if you started before you picked up this book, for instance – then congratulations! You've reclaimed ninety minutes out of your day. That adds up to one workday per week. Even at a conservative estimate, that's more than a month per year. Your year now has twelve months in it, not eleven, like it did before.

What are you going to do with all this new-found time? How about books? How about reading long-form newspaper and magazine articles, especially those written by genuine experts? What about a decent online course? This will help you understand the underlying mechanisms of the world. Go deep, not broad. Engage with content that is truly relevant and overlaps with your circle of competence. If you're wondering what a circle of competence is, don't worry: we'll take a closer look in Chapter 9. For now, though, it's enough to know that your circle of competence is your niche, the area where your competence is well above average (or where you're striving to make it above average). Essentially, your field of expertise.

What about thinking? Ever since he founded Microsoft, Bill Gates has dedicated a full week twice a year to sheer thought. He calls it 'Think Week'. He packs a suitcase full of books and a stack of notepaper and goes off the grid. You should do the same. After all, you've reclaimed four weeks a year. It doesn't have to be a private island. A remote cabin in the woods will do just as well! Few of us have the luxury of getting away, but even if we don't have a cabin in the woods for two solitary weeks, there are ways to find similar calm in our daily lives.

As soon as a piece of news is in the world, it becomes public knowledge and you will not enjoy an advantage in knowing about it. You will, however, gain a huge advantage over your peers and competitors if firstly you have a deeper awareness of the background context and secondly, if that context is *not* widely disseminated. And you will only reach this awareness through intensive reading and thought.

During the initial stage of abstinence, in those first thirty days, you'll have to literally *force* yourself not to consume any news. The impulse will be there, but your willpower is stronger. After a while, the urge itself will subside. You won't need as much willpower, because you won't even want to read the news. This means you've reached stage two.

By the third stage you'll have developed an outright aversion to the news. You'll automatically turn your head away from the headlines reaching out to you from abandoned newspapers, at newsstands or on public screens. If you've achieved stage three, congratulations once more! You're now officially clean – and you've won your life back.

6

THE SOFT OPTION

If my suggestions seem too radical, then let me recommend the soft option. It works like this: avoid the daily papers (print and online) completely, as well as radio, TV and the stream of news on social media. Instead, read one weekly paper or magazine. One. Read it in print form, not online – for the simple reason that the printed paper contains no hyperlinks. Hyperlinks are problematic for two reasons. First, you've got to decide each time whether or not to click the link, costing you time, attention and a degree of willpower. Second, if you do click on the link, it takes you away from the actual article, and you're immediately lost in the wilds of the internet, tossed to and fro like a piece of flotsam.

Read your chosen weekly in one go. Don't divvy up your reading into several sittings and definitely don't spread it across several days. Best of all, set a time limit, let's say sixty minutes, for the entire paper. Set a timer. That way you'll minimise the damaging impact of the news on your brain and your psyche. Which newspapers are ideal? Those that are the least sensationalist and the least reliant on advertising. But, as I said, choose only one.

Your next step will be to winnow down your reading to a fixed number of articles per edition. I have a few friends who exclusively read the *Economist*, and exclusively the feature articles (usually four or five of them, under the heading 'Leaders'). Others read the main feature in the German weekly magazine *Der Spiegel* and ignore everything else. Others still restrict themselves to just the main editorial, or an op-ed in a weekend edition. Ideally you want to choose a news segment that doesn't change format week on week, or changes only slightly, and is always on the same page.

Maybe you're afraid of missing something important? Let me reassure you. If you read the feature piece in *Der Spiegel* every week, you'll read fifty-two articles per year. All the major events of the year will be covered.

After you've done the soft version for a few months, you may be ready for the more radical approach. If so, I'd recommend an intermediate stage: when the latest edition of your weekly appears in the letterbox, put it unread into a drawer and instead read an edition that's at least a month old. The broad topics your friends are discussing (the war in Syria, the trade war, Brexit, whatever) will doubtless be mentioned there, too. By reading an older edition you minimise the danger of being sucked back into the news whirlpool while maintaining the comforting sense of not missing out. You'll grow more confident about avoiding the news.

Still, be warned: the soft route is much more dangerous than the radical one, because you'll be sailing hard into the wind. The siren call of the news media will be much louder, sweeter and more alluring. If you dare – and I hope you do

– then simply choose the radical path straight off the bat: outright cold turkey.

What should you do when you suffer a relapse? I experienced one myself, when Donald Trump was elected to the US presidency in 2016 and I found myself suddenly caught up in election fever. I started consulting news websites every day, until finally I realised that all it was doing was getting me riled up, and that I couldn't do anything to change the situation. Soon I was yet again experiencing all the negative effects I will describe in the following chapters: anxiety, cognitive errors, time-wasting. I also felt bad because I'd broken my own resolution. My sense of equilibrium had taken two big hits. After exactly four weeks I switched the tap back off. So – what should you do if you relapse? The same thing an alcoholic would: simply start again, reinstituting a zero-tolerance policy.

You could simply close this book right now and banish the news from your life – and you would rapidly experience for yourself how positive this is for your mind and body. If you need more convincing, however – or you need to persuade others – then read on. I have a whole arsenal of arguments against consuming the news. And now, of course, you actually have time to read them – now you're no longer being distracted.

7

NEWS IS IRRELEVANT: PART 1

You've probably devoured roughly 20,000 news items in the past twelve months, approximately sixty per day at a conservative estimate. Be honest with yourself, can you think of a single one that helped you make a better decision about your life, your family, your career, your well-being or your business? A decision you wouldn't have made without the news? None of the friends to whom I asked this question could give me more than two examples – from 20,000. That's a pretty shoddy hit rate! Surveying the last ten years, during which time I've been news-free, I can think of only one piece of news that would have been genuinely helpful to read. In 2010, I drove to the airport, only to discover that my flight had been cancelled due to a volcanic eruption in Iceland.

When it comes to the things that really matter in your life, the news is irrelevant. Best-case scenario, it's entertaining, but otherwise useless. It takes a degree of effort to make this mental step.

But let's suppose that, against all expectations, you *did* read a news report that improved your quality of life – without which you would have been worse off. How much rubbish did your brain have to cope with in order to unearth this one truffle?

I know what you're thinking. *You don't have to be so black and white about this. There's a middle ground here: just be more selective about what you read. Only consume articles that are worth something and leave everything else aside.* It sounds good in theory but doesn't work in practice. Why? Because we can't judge the value of a news report in advance. To adequately judge whether a headline is worth reading, we've actually got to read it – and soon we're back to sampling the whole buffet.

Perhaps we can leave the selection process to the professionals? How good are journalists at tracking down and filtering important events? The first internet browser appeared on 11 November 1993 – probably the most significant invention of the twentieth century, after the atomic bomb and the discovery of antibiotics. Do you know what that browser was called? Mosaic. If you didn't know the answer, you have a good excuse: it didn't make the news. What were the lead stories on German television that day? Party funding was being reformed. The Israeli prime minister had a meeting with Bill Clinton. The Pope had fractured his shoulder. My point is that neither journalists nor consumers have much sense of what's relevant.

The relationship between relevance and media attention seems inverse: the greater the fanfare in the news, the smaller the relevance of the event. Over the years I've come to the conclusion that the items journalists *don't* report on are usually the very things you actually want to know!

Acknowledging the possible irrelevance of the news is nothing new. In Tolstoy's masterpiece *Anna Karenina*, published in 1877, Sergei Ivanovich observes that 'the newspapers published a great deal that was superfluous and exaggerated, with the sole aim of attracting attention and talking one another down.'

Relevance is a highly personal issue. It's not defined by the government or the Pope, or by your boss or your therapist. And don't get it confused with the media's perspective. To the media, what's relevant is anything that grabs attention. This is the racket at the heart of the industry's business model. The news they supply us is irrelevant, but it's sold as relevant. 'The relevant versus the new': it's the fundamental battle facing us today.

If I were going to put together a current affairs programme personally tailored to me, what would it look like? It would include the following: a status report on my family. What have my kids been up to? What's on their minds? What's on my wife's mind? A look back at the things I could have done better that day – a sort of daily critique. A health check on my family. A status report on my aunt's illness. The physical and psychological condition of my friends. An update on the planned traffic-calming measures in my town. The waste pick-up schedule. A renovation project in the kitchen. Holiday plans. My email exchange with a researcher. The plans for my next novel. A new business idea. A review of a pleasant conversation I had at lunch. An article on the neighbourhood, the school, the city – in other words, regional and hyper-regional news. And all the things I need for my job as a writer.

Would my personal show be a hit with anyone else? Obviously not. What's relevant to me has absolutely nothing to do with what's relevant for other people, let alone with what's on the global news. Most people assume that the 'world news' is automatically relevant to them. They are mistaken.

News organisations want you to believe they're giving you a competitive advantage. Plenty of people fall for this. In fact, consuming the news is far from a competitive advantage; it actively *disadvantages* you. If it did genuinely help you to get ahead, news journalists would be the highest earners in the world. But they're not – at all. It can be hard to assess exactly what makes people successful, but we do know with some certainty what hinders them, and the plethora of news titbits is definitely on the list.

8

NEWS IS IRRELEVANT: PART 2
(A THOUGHT EXPERIMENT)

It's sheer chance that our planet's diameter is the size it is. Let's imagine the earth measured twice as much in diameter, giving a surface area that's four times the size of the actual figure. Assuming the same population density, there would be four times the number of people living on the planet. The cities and countryside would be hardly any different from those on our world. Your life, dear reader, would feel exactly the same (okay, ignoring the change in gravity). One thing, however, would be different: the news.

There would be roughly four times as much 'important news' on the larger planet than on ours. At least four times as many heroic people, psychopaths, scandals, collapsing bridges, musical geniuses, murders, traffic pile-ups, celebs, divorces, volcanic eruptions, tsunamis, tweets, shark attacks, terrorist threats, computer viruses, bursting dams, environmental catastrophes, bank robberies, armed conflicts, PR reports, inventions, start-ups and bankruptcies.

This information, however, would not necessarily increase proportionally, at least not in areas governed by a 'winner takes all' approach. There would continue to be only one Nobel Prize per year per subject area, for instance – not four.

Only one person would be the richest in the world – not four. There would be only one female shot-put gold medallist at the Olympics – not four. There might be twice as many brands of cars, social networks and search engines, but probably not four times as many. News from other areas, however, would disproportionately *increase*: with four times the population, there could be ten times the number of heroic acts of cooperation or scandalous conflicts, left-field company mergers and court judgements. There would be many more flight connections and instabilities in the financial system. Yet let's stick with the number four, for simplicity's sake (this is a thought experiment, after all).

If we want to claim, therefore, that the news you consume today is mostly relevant, on a larger planet you'd logically have to consume four times the amount of 'relevant' news. Instead of ninety minutes per day you'd have to invest six hours per day. Clearly, you wouldn't do that. You'd limit your consumption to a level that's more compatible with the other demands of your everyday life. After all, you have a job and a family, friends, a pet and hobbies. Now, this means that when push comes to shove you'd be prepared to limit yourself to a quarter of ostensibly 'crucial' news. This wouldn't pose a problem. I'm sure you've guessed my question here: if you're willing to cut down in the thought experiment, then why not in real life? No news is so important that you can't live without it.

Still worried about missing 'something important'? In my experience, when something truly important happens, you hear about it even if you're living in a protected news-cocoon. When a pipe bursts in your basement, you hear about it from an attentive neighbour. And if a terrorist blows up a bus somewhere in the world, you'll find out. Big news will inevitably leak out and find you. If you hear it from family, friends and colleagues you'll even have the added benefit of meta-information: you know the priorities and world views of your friends, so you'll know how to evaluate your sources. And if somehow you don't hear about the bus attack, it doesn't matter. On the contrary, you should be pleased. Worse things may be happening on other planets, and we are comfortable remaining in the dark.

For the most part, you'll find out about truly relevant events by reading good books. After all, non-fiction books are basically just ultra-long, elaborately planned and researched articles. Of course, books don't appear on the day something happens. But this doesn't matter – vanishingly few events are time-sensitive for you. Information given on the day something happens is necessarily basic and inadequate. And in fact, what we want is context and consideration, which is what you get from books – even it arrives a few months or a year late.

9

NEWS IS OUTSIDE YOUR
CIRCLE OF COMPETENCE

What does relevance mean in concrete terms? There are two definitions. In the narrower, hard sense something is relevant when it enables you to make better decisions. In the wider sense, anything that allows you to understand the world better is relevant.

The legendary investor Warren Buffett uses the wonderful term *circle of competence*. Anything inside this circle is an area of expertise. Anything outside it is something you don't understand, or don't fully understand. Buffett's motto is as follows: 'Know your circle of competence and stick within it. The size of that circle is not very important; knowing its boundaries, however, is vital.' Tom Watson, the founder of IBM, is living proof of this thesis. He has said of himself, 'I'm no genius. I'm smart in spots – but I stay around those spots.'

Organise your professional life rigorously around your circle of competence. This radical focus will bear more than monetary fruits. Above all you'll save time, because you won't keep having to decide where to direct your attention. Knowing your circle of competence is your tool, your scalpel, enabling you to divide sources of information into what's valuable and what's not.

In concrete terms? All the information that matches your circle of competence is valuable. Everything that's outside your circle of competence is best ignored. Thinking about it will only waste your time and affect your concentration.

Over the course of your life you will modify your circle of competence. You may even add extra areas of interest. In these cases, creating a deep knowledge base by reading textbooks and completing online courses, reading long articles and talking to people in the know is imperative.

So what's the big deal about this circle of competence? These days – with very few exceptions – you'll only find professional success in a niche. The greater your knowledge and the greater your ability within that niche, the greater your success. If you're the best in the world within your niche, you've made it. This is related to the 'winner takes all' effect I described in *The Art of the Good Life*. Simply put, you have a choice: nerd or loser.

At first blush, 'nerd' sounds terrible. But you could just as well call it 'mastery'. Sounds a bit more appealing, doesn't it? Beethoven was a nerd, but what a nerd: he was the best in the world at composing symphonies. Outside his circle of competence, however, he wasn't outstanding at anything. Picasso was a nerd. Yuri Gagarin, the first man in space, was a nerd. Isaac Newton, probably the greatest scientist of all time, was a nerd. Outside his circle of competence he was a dead loss: he managed to ruin himself financially by speculating on the stock market.

With a sharply defined circle of competence, it
easy to decide what information belongs in your brain and
what belongs in the rubbish. Let's say you're a heart
surgeon. Pertinent scientific journals will be an area of
focus for you. Perhaps also leadership magazines and
books, if you lead a team. Everything else you can safely
ignore. You don't need to know whether one president
shook another one's hand. You don't need to know whether
two trains crashed somewhere in the world. Your brain is
already full. The more you cram it with junk, the less room
there is for the information you genuinely need to know.

Let's say you're an architect. Obviously, you too should
be reading professional magazines and books on your
subject. You'll have to keep up to date on any current and
planned changes to building regulations. How you receive
that information will vary from place to place, but you definitely won't find it on a general news website. You might
also read magazines and books that keep you informed on
the latest word in aesthetics and design. True, these professional journals can be quite expensive. Relevance costs
money. What you don't need to know is whether China has
sent a space probe to Mars, so save yourself the time.

Say, you need to have surgery (brain, liver, heart, whatever). And under your particular health system you can
pick one of two doctors. Both doctors have the same IQ.
Both have studied at the same university. Both have the
same number of years of experience. Both are nice and
friendly. Doctor A consumes news like the average person
(ninety minutes per day). The time Doctor A spends on
reading the news, doctor B spends reading the latest

scientific journals and attending conferences pertaining to his circle of competence. Which doctor would you pick? The news-junkie doctor? I doubt it.

Everybody's circle of competence contains a few sources of specialised media that you absolutely need to read. Go deep, not broad. What's outside your circle of competence, however, you're best off giving a miss. Should you use Google? If the information you're googling is relevant to your circle of competence, then sure. The internet is full of valuable information. But be on your guard: don't get side-tracked and end up bogged down in stuff that's entertaining but irrelevant.

You now hold a scalpel in your hand: use it to separate the relevant from the irrelevant. When you consistently organise your life around your circle of competence, you'll realise that ninety-nine per cent of what you read, see and hear in the media is irrelevant to you. Slice it off.

10

NEWS GETS RISK
ASSESSMENT ALL WRONG

Our central nervous system reacts disproportionately strongly to visible, scandalous, sensationalist, shocking, personal, loud, striking, polarising, rapidly changing, colourful stimuli – and disproportionately weakly to abstract, ambivalent, complex, slowly developing, inter-related pieces of information that require some degree of interpretation. Producers of the news systematically exploit this distortion in our perspective.

The news media, whether big or small, is obsessed with the immediate. Gripping stories, shrieking images, shock-ing videos and astonishing 'facts' grab our attention. This is how their business model works. The adverts that finance the whole circus will only be sold if they're going to be seen: if they're surrounded by garish news stories. The upshot? Anything subtle, complex and abstract, anything that develops slowly and is remotely abstruse, will be systematically dismissed by the media, and by ourselves, despite being the content that actually matters more to our lives and genuinely furthers our understanding of the world. Tax-payer-funded, advert-free media such as the BBC can afford to take the high road. But they are not completely free of the 'circus' as inevitably they find themselves in competition with private media companies for viewership and advertising revenue.

Let's take the following event: a car drives over a bridge and the bridge collapses. What does the news media focus on? The car. The person in the car. Where they came from. Where they were going. How they felt during the accident (assuming they survived it). What kind of person they are (or were, before the accident). Of course, what happened to this person is tragic, but to us – given that we don't know them – is it relevant? Not remotely. What's relevant to us is the bridge! The structural stability of the bridge. Whether there are other bridges constructed in the same way and from the same materials, and if so, where those bridges are. That's what actually matters – so that no one else gets injured. Not the car, or its driver. Any car could have caused the bridge to collapse. Perhaps even a strong wind or a dog trotting over it could have been enough. So why does the news media report on the crumpled car? Because it looks so marvellously horrible; because they can connect the story to a person – and because this story is cheap to produce.

Another example: an employee at the tax office commits fraud, costing the city a million pounds. The media will pounce on the man. They'll comb through his background and his private life. What was his upbringing like? What motivated him? What was going on in his mind? What was his relationship like with his bosses? His colleagues? But the man himself is a red herring. There are two important elements to this story: risk management and company culture at the tax office. These are what's relevant. Sloppy risk management and an accordingly lax company culture will always breed a few people willing to commit fraud; their life stories are beside the point.

As news junkies, we walk around with an entirely false sense of risk. We make the same mistake in other areas, too. Terrorism is overplayed, chronic stress is downplayed. A banking collapse is overplayed, government debt is downplayed. The antics of the Kardashians are overplayed, the results of atmospheric research are downplayed.

Astronauts are overplayed, nurses are downplayed. Shark attacks are overplayed, ocean acidification is downplayed. Plane crashes are overplayed, antibiotic-resistant bacteria are downplayed. Changes in tax laws are overplayed, changes in interest rates are downplayed. Politicians are overplayed, teachers are downplayed. Heads of state are overplayed, diplomats are underplayed. Opinions are overplayed, actions are downplayed.

Consuming the news day after day skews our sense of what's important. It gives us a far-from-realistic assessment, leading to inappropriate, systematically incorrect behaviour. The risks you read about in the press aren't the ones you need to worry about. A not-insignificant number of people who see a plane crash on TV stop flying for a while – even though these events are extremely rare and do not justify such a fundamental shift in behaviour.

Surely it's enough to be aware of this fact, I hear you say, and bear it in mind as we consume the news? Wrong. We can't compensate for this tendency to overplay gripping stories with deliberate contemplation and sensible assessment. Our brains are too weak. They can't cope with the distinction. Even bankers and economists, who have tremendous incentive to assess risk realistically, aren't able to do so. By now you'll have realised that there's only one solution: disconnect completely from the news. Don't try to outsmart your skewed perception of risk. Just get rid of it.

11

NEWS IS A WASTE OF TIME

The news comes at an exorbitant price because it's a waste of time. First, there's the time you actually spend consuming the news: reading, listening, watching or scrolling through content on your phone or laptop. Second, it takes time to refocus your attention, known as the 'switching cost': you lose time going back to whatever you were doing before you were distracted by the news. Third, the news impairs your focus long after you've consumed it. Stories and images end up haunting you hours later, persistently interrupting your train of thought.

Let's do a quick calculation. You flick through the morning paper, listen to the radio news at lunchtime, then watch the evening round-up on TV. Count up all those brief detours to your favourite news websites when work gets stressful and you treat yourself to a break. Add all those innocent little peeks at your smartphone and social-media news feeds, the ones you use as a 'reward'. The sum total is the entirety of the time you spend actually consuming the news. The Pew Research Center – an American think tank that canvasses public opinion – estimates this figure to be between fifty-eight and ninety-six minutes per day. And the higher your level of education, the higher your daily news consumption.

Now factor in the time it takes you to refocus. You have to gather your thoughts every single time. Where exactly did you leave off? Where did you save that document? What was the next thing you were going to do, before the news hogged your attention? Refocusing alone robs you of two or three minutes each and every time.

Maybe you also take two five-minute periods to brood on a story you can't let go – the pictures of a train accident, perhaps. All in all, this comes to at least an hour and a half per day.

Even if we're being generous, that's a month per year. My year still has twelve months, while yours (if you consume the news) only has eleven. Why would you do that to yourself? What do you really have to show for all this lost time? Do you understand the world better? Have you expanded your circle of competence? Do you make better decisions? Has your concentration improved? Do you have more peace of mind?

From a global perspective, this loss of time is immense. Take the terrorist attacks in Mumbai in 2008. In their bid for attention, terrorists killed one hundred and sixty-six people. Imagine that a billion people focused their attention on the tragedy in Mumbai for an hour on average: they followed the news and watched various 'commentators' babbling about it on TV. It's entirely feasible, given India alone has more than a billion inhabitants. Indeed, many of them may well have spent the whole day watching the drama unfold. But let's stick with a conservative estimate. A billion people being distracted for an hour equals a billion hours of distraction, more than a hundred thousand years. The average global life expectancy is sixty-six years. In economic terms, then, consuming the news 'wasted' two thousand human lives, more than ten times than died in the attack. In a sense, the news organisations became the terrorists' unwitting accomplices. Of course, it may seem inappropriate to compare victims of terrorism with victims of news consumption, but the sad truth is that terrorists need the media. (More on this in Chapter 28.) The situation was even more extreme when Michael Jackson died: although what happened was tragic for Jackson's relatives and his most dedicated fans, for most of us it was completely unimportant – and yet we squandered millions of hours on it.

Information these days is no longer a scarce resource – attention, on the other hand, is in short supply. So why are we so irresponsible with it? I doubt you're so profligate with your health, your reputation or your money. Two thousand years ago, Seneca wondered the same thing: when it comes to money, the great philosopher pondered, we're tight-fisted. Yet when it comes to our time, we're as spendthrift as can be – even though time is the only commodity with which we really ought to be miserly.

Over the course of my life I've read countless books on time management and tried out dozens of their well-meaning suggestions. Yet I have come to the conclusion that, for all the strategies and techniques they suggest, there is no easier and more productive method of reclaiming time than giving up the news.

12

NEWS OBSCURES
THE BIG PICTURE

The news is incapable of explaining anything. Its brief reports are like tiny, shimmering soap bubbles bursting on the surface of a complex world. It's all the more absurd, then, that news corporations pride themselves on accurately reporting the facts. These facts are usually no more than the consequences and side effects of deeper underlying causes. Even if you gobble down the latest images and reports from Syria every single day, it won't get you one jot further towards understanding the war. There's actually an inverse relationship: the more images and front-line dispatches raining down on you, the less you'll understand what's going on in the war and why. News corporations and consumers both fall prey to the same mistake, confusing the presentation of facts with insight into the functional context of the world. 'Facts, facts and more facts': this is the marginalising credo of nearly all news corporations.

We ought to try and understand the 'generators' underlying these events. We ought to be investigating the 'engine room' behind them. Sadly, shockingly few journalists are able to explain these causal relationships, because the processes that shape cultural, intellectual, economic, military, political and environmental events are mostly invisible. They are complex, non-linear and hard for our brains to digest. This is why news corporations focus on the easy stuff: anecdotes, scandals, celebrity gossip and natural disasters. They are cheap to produce and easy to digest.

Worse still, the few journalists who do understand the 'engine room' and are capable of writing about it aren't given the space to do so – let alone time to think. Why? Because the bulk of readers would rather consume ten juicy morsels of news than a single thorough article. Ten lurid little scandals generate more attention – and thus more advertising revenue – than one intelligent article of the same length.

You probably remember puzzle books from childhood that featured pages and pages containing nothing but numbered dots. The game was to connect the dots in order, and gradually an image would appear. News reports are nothing but dots – and nobody has made the effort to connect them and solve the puzzle. No matter how many you consume, no image will ever emerge.

To see the bigger picture, you need the connecting lines. You need the context, the mutual dependencies, the feedback, the immediate repercussions – and the consequences of these repercussions. News is the opposite of understanding the world. It suggests there are only events – events without context.

Yet the opposite is true: nearly everything that happens in the world is complex. Implying these events are singular phenomena is a lie – a lie promulgated by news producers because it tickles our palates. This is a disaster: consuming the news to 'understand the world' is worse than not consuming any news at all. Thomas Jefferson, one of the Founding Fathers of the USA, realised this as early as 1807: 'The man who never looks into a newspaper is better informed than he who reads them.' Facts get in the way of thought. Your brain can drown in facts. If you consume the news, you'll be under the *illusion* that you understand the world. This illusion can lead to overconfidence.

In one famous study, Professor Paul Slovic of the University of Oregon tested the impact of data on horse-race betting. He gave an increasing number of data points about the horses to the people betting, then asked them not only which horse they thought would win the race but also how confident they were about the accuracy of their prediction. The result? The wealth of information on the individual horses (all obvious stuff) had no effect on the accuracy of their predictions but a massive impact on their confidence. The necessary caution, scepticism and modesty were all washed away by the flood of information. Careful predictions mutated into sure-fire convictions.

You, dear reader, do not want to fall victim to this glut of news. You know the quality of your decision-making will be reduced by 'facts, facts and more facts'. If you give up the news, you'll accept for the first time that you might not understand the world. You'll be more modest when it comes to your knowledge, more cautious, more considered, and you won't fall victim to overconfidence.

'Nobody knows what's happening. The newspapers only pretend as though they do from day to day,' wrote the shrewd Swiss playwright Max Frisch more than forty years ago. Current events cast a shadow on understanding. It's best to avoid the daily news completely. Read books and long articles that do justice to the complexity of the world – no sparkling headlines. No founts of facts. No points without connections. After a few months, you'll be rewarded with a clearer understanding of the world.

13

NEWS IS TOXIC TO YOUR BODY

Imagine two hypothetical species of animal. The brain of Species A reacts primarily to negative information. The brain of Species B, on the other hand, is more active when receiving positive information. Who has a better life? Species B, of course; while the As are perpetually stressed and unhappy, the Bs enjoy the sunny side of existence. They take pleasure in all the beautiful things they see and hear, and simply laugh off all the negativity. Who will live longer? Species A, of course. The Bs, enviable as their sunny psychology might be, will be wiped from the gene pool within a few months. Only the As will survive. Survival demands constant wariness; it demands oversensitivity to negative information. We are Species A.

Bad news is perceived as more relevant than good news. Negative information has twice the impact that positive information does. In psychology, this is called *negativity bias*, and it can be observed in even one-year-old infants. They respond more sensitively to negative stimuli than to positive ones. Adults are no different. A stock falling by ten per cent makes us twice as unhappy as a stock climbing by ten per cent makes us happy. *Negativity bias* is innate. The news media hasn't inculcated into us our weakness for negative information; it simply exploits this weakness in expert fashion, delivering a stream of shocking stories that are tailor-made for our anxious brains.

The news continually stimulates our sympathetic nervous system, a part of our autonomic nervous system. Psychological stressors lead to the release of adrenaline by the hypothalamus. Adrenaline then leads to a rise in cortisol. So, every garish story can lead to the production of this stress hormone. Cortisol floods our bloodstream, weakening the immune system and inhibiting the production of growth hormones. By consuming the news, you're putting your body under stress. Chronic stress leads to anxiety and digestive and growth problems and leaves us prone to infection. Other potential side effects of news consumption include panic attacks, aggression, tunnel vision and emotional desensitisation. In short, consuming the news puts your psychological and physical health at risk.

According to a study by the American Psychological Association, half of all adults suffer from the symptoms of stress caused by news consumption. This is unsurprising. After all, in the last ten years two things have changed radically. First, we consume far more news than previously – thanks to our omnipresent mobile phones, and, in some countries news screens in many public places. One in ten Americans checks the world news once an hour. The figure for social-media feeds is even higher. Second, the news is becoming ever more garish and shocking. Graham Davey, Professor Emeritus of Psychology at Sussex University and editor-in-chief of the *Journal of Experimental Psychopathology*, confirms that these two changes often have detrimental effects on the mental health of people who consume the news. Some videos are so intense that they can trigger acute symptoms like sleep disruption, mood swings, aggressive behaviour or even PTSD. 'The way that news is presented and the way that we access news has changed significantly over the last fifteen to twenty years', says Graham Davey. 'These changes have often been detrimental to general mental health.'

We all have our anxieties. Sometimes they overwhelm us and make us incapable of action. In a healthy living environment, there are all sorts of tricks to help us cope with these difficult situations better (which I described in *The Art of the Good Life*). For example, taking stock of your anxieties, writing them down one by one, and then deciding if you have the power or opportunity to do anything about these issues or not. It's an exercise learned from the Stoics of ancient Rome. There are things you can influence and things that you cannot. There is no point getting worked up about things you cannot change. For example, there is nothing I can do about my past or about a Trump tweet. So why let it make me anxious?

Unfortunately, consuming the news can thwart these coping methods. Davey has shown that negative television reports intensify personal anxiety, even when the anxiety-generating content on TV is completely unrelated to your personal situation.

Living healthily takes willpower. The willpower to think clearly, work productively, eat nutritiously and keep your body moving. Unfortunately, willpower is depleted as stress increases. This leads to procrastination. You replace unpleasant but important activities with unimportant ones. You may, for example, substitute a trip to the gym with surfing online news sites. Now we're in a vicious cycle: consuming the news leads to chronic stress, stress saps willpower, and a lack of willpower makes us more likely to spend longer online, which in turn leads to more stress and further depletes our willpower.

The upshot is clear: consuming the news reduces your quality of life. You will be more stressed, more on edge, more susceptible to disease, and you'll die earlier. That's an especially sad piece of news – but one that does, at least, deserve your attention.

14

NEWS CONFIRMS
OUR MISTAKES

We're prone to approximately a hundred and twenty systematic cognitive errors, which I described in my book *The Art of Thinking Clearly*. We regularly deviate from the principles of rationality, sensible thought and action. These errors reduce the quality of our decision-making in our private and professional lives, and the news – far from enlightening us – actually reinforces them.

Let's take the granddaddy of all cognitive errors, *confirmation bias*. Ask yourself: 'What's the next number after 3, 6, 9, 12?' If you're like most people, you'll say '15'. Yet you could have said '14' or '52' with equal justification. 'But wait,' you'll probably object, 'the rule here is clearly to keep adding three!' It might be, but that's not necessarily so. The rule could equally be this: 'The next number must be bigger than the previous one.' So what happened here? The neat intervals of three caught your eye; you let yourself be captivated by them and they blinded you to all other possibilities.

This is entirely normal behaviour. We automatically block out clues that contradict our favourite opinions and are oversensitive to news that confirms our beliefs. This is fine for strings of numbers. It's rather more dangerous, however, when it comes to political views or money. We're masters of interpreting new information so that it remains consonant with our previous point of view. The more news you consume, the more frequently you'll come across confirmatory information, even if your opinions are false. These days the news no longer functions as a test probe, poking holes in inaccurate opinions (as was formerly the case, when there wasn't much news around); rather, it cements them.

Confirmation bias is most dangerous of all when it comes to ideologies. Ideologies are among the stupidest things our brains have ever produced. They are essentially self-built mental prisons. Ideologies are opinions to the power of ten: they bundle opinions, as it were, and constitute whole world views. Their effect on the brain is like a high-voltage current, causing all sorts of impulsive actions and blowing every fuse. Avoid ideologies and dogmas at any price. Ideologies narrow your world view and lead you to make terrible decisions. News, in reinforcing confirmation bias, becomes ideology's accomplice. We can see exactly this happening in political discourse: if you unleash a whirlwind of news on the population, it polarises the public.

So far, so clear. The problem, however, is that people don't realise when they've fallen prey to an ideology. If you meet someone who shows signs of a dogmatic infestation, ask them the following question: 'Tell me what specific facts you would have to learn in order to change your mind.' If they don't have an answer, then give that person a wide berth. Do the same for their opinions.

A word of caution here: don't get smug. Ask yourself precisely the same question if you suspect you've edged too close to a particular dogma. Actively search for counter-arguments. Imagine you're on a TV talk show with five other guests, all of whom are arguing your counterpoint. Only when you can defend your own position against five well-founded opposing arguments have you really earned your opinion.

But even if your brain hasn't been corroded by an ideology, and you simply have certain theories about the world, the stock market, your neighbour's dog, your boss's soul, your competitors' strategies – which is perfectly normal – even then, confirmation bias can strike. Consuming the news amplifies this human weakness even in its milder forms. Why? Because in an endless stream of news we can always find enough to cement our theories, no matter how wrong they are. As a consequence we get hubristic, put our mental blinkers on, take idiotic risks and miss out on great opportunities.

15

NEWS REINFORCES
HINDSIGHT BIAS

The world is in a complex, dynamic process of chaos. Cause and effect don't hang together in a linear fashion. In almost all cases, the interplay of hundreds or even thousands of causes lead to a particular event, yet this event is often attributed to only a few.

Take the financial crisis of 2008. A whole poisonous cocktail of circumstances was responsible for the collapse of the financial system: euphoria at the stock exchange, high levels of private mortgage credit, the worldwide conviction that house prices could never fall, the banks' debt-to-equity ratio, synthetic securities (with such cryptic names as 'mortgage-backed securities' and 'collateralised debt obligations'), and insuring these securities, the criminal behaviour of the rating agencies, the criminal behaviour of the mortgage sellers, the vastly excessive appetite of European investors for American bonds, lax oversight on both sides of the Atlantic, the unsuitable risk equations, the quasi-governmental guarantees and so on.

In hindsight, this all seems so clear. It gives us the illusion that these crises are comprehensible – and predictable. This is called *hindsight bias*. But in the eye of the hurricane, nothing whatsoever was clear. And, sadly, when we're embroiled in the next crisis, things won't be any clearer then either.

Of course, we would also fall prey to hindsight bias without the news, but it does amplify this cognitive error. The shorter the news report, the more dangerous it is.

News has to be extremely short even as it tells a story. This can only be done through a brutal process of simplification. No matter what happened – a straightforward bicycle accident or a worldwide financial crisis – it will only ever be attributed to one or two causes. Nothing will be said of the dozens of other causes, the interplay between them, or the retroactive effects playing out between the event and its causes (intensifying or dampening effects). In this way consumers are given the illusion that the world is simpler and more explicable than it actually is, and the quality of their decision-making suffers.

If you avoid the news and instead either read long articles and books on a particular topic or discuss it with experts, you'll get a much more realistic picture of the situation. And you won't fall prey to the illusion that the future is easy to understand.

This is easier said than done, because our brains are desperate for stories that 'make sense' as quickly and simply as possible. Whether they correspond to reality is irrelevant. News journalists are keen to provide us with these pseudo-stories. Instead of reporting that the stock market has fallen by one per cent, the reporter tells us: 'The market has fallen by one per cent *because of X*.' Here, X is usually a familiar factor: changing profit forecasts, fears about the euro, the publication of employment statistics, a decision issued by the central bank, a terrorist attack, a transport strike, a handshake between two presidents, whatever. The fact is, however, that this sole 'X' does not exist. Since the news is so telescoped, it's necessarily a bullshit explanation.

It reminds me of my schooldays. My history textbook listed three reasons (not two, not seven) for why the French Revolution happened. Yet these three reasons were only a fraction of the true causes. We don't know for certain what caused the French Revolution, much less why it was precipitated specifically in 1789. Nor do we know why the stock market is changing the way it's changing. There are too many factors at play. We don't know for sure why a war breaks out, why a technological breakthrough happens or why Barcelona won the game against Madrid. Any journalist who writes 'The market fell *because of* X' or 'The company went bankrupt *because of* Y' is either an idiot or trying to pull the wool over their readers' eyes. True, X and Y may well have had a causal impact, but this is far from proven – and other influences may well have been much more significant. News reports are often sold as 'analysis', when in fact they're merely anecdotes.

Resist the temptation to explain the world so cheaply. You're holding yourself back from real, serious reflection – and robbing yourself of your only chance to understand the world at least fractionally better.

16

NEWS REINFORCES
AVAILABILITY BIAS

Quick, name a flower, a colour, a pet!

Finished? If you're wired like most people, you'll have said 'rose', 'red' and 'dog' or 'cat', even though there are tens of thousands of different types of flowers, several dozen colours and at least a hundred different kinds of pet. This is *availability bias*. We think of what's right in front of our noses – or what's already in our brains.

What is available has a strong influence on our decision-making. Every decision is based on something, and this something consists of information. For the sake of convenience, we always draw on what's to hand from the pool of available information, rather than on things that might be more important but would need to be researched first. Let's take an example from business: the management goes through the points on the day's agenda as submitted by the CEO, not through points that might be more important but *aren't* on the agenda. For example, they might discuss at length a ten per cent reduction in parking spaces at their headquarters, because it's on the agenda; but not a competitor that might threaten ten per cent of the company's revenue. Or, here's an example from politics: I live in Bern, the capital of Switzerland. It's not an especially big city, so you unavoidably end up meeting people who work for the government. One senior civil servant told me that at weekly briefings the ministers all wanted to discuss the latest press reports first. It got tedious, he said, because he always had to point out that there were actually more important topics to consider. The news has a tremendous ability to jostle to the forefront of our minds. This makes it nearly impossible to make sensible decisions – especially in business and politics.

If you consume the news, you run the risk of using it as the basis of your decision-making, even if it has virtually nothing to do with the matter at hand. This can happen quite subconsciously: you may be listening to news about a plane crash on the other side of the world, for instance, then the following day you get the opportunity to fly to London and seal a potential deal. You don't get on the plane and so the meeting falls through, even though the crash on the news had nothing to do with your flight to London.

The news makes itself comfortable in our brains – and we love to wallow in it. The more emotional the imagery, video clips and headlines, the more space it takes up. The news puts itself at the top of our mental filing cabinet and is thus much more available than other information – statistics, historical comparisons, complex arguments and counterarguments – which might be a much better basis for making a decision.

Those who set the agenda wield power over the discussion. If you let news journalists decide what you should think about, you're giving them far too much power over your life. Surely you, dear reader, would rather be in the cockpit? Don't hand over the controls to a bunch of stressed-out hacks. They happily confuse 'unavailable' with 'non-existent' because they have neither the budget nor the time to seek out the most valuable information. And this error is passed on automatically to consumers.

News journalists also labour under a second grave misconception: they confuse 'prevented' with 'non-existent'. Heroic acts that prevented accidents – that pre-empted disaster – are largely invisible to them. It's easy to dispatch a reporter to the next fire, but it's not so easy to send one to cover a fire that was *prevented* by judicious behaviour, even though fighting fire is much less effective than pre-empting it. Nassim Taleb uses a different example: let's imagine someone had convinced the American aviation authorities to install bulletproof cockpit doors and locks into planes, thereby avoiding an attack like that of 11 September 2001. Not a single journalist would have reported on this person or their brilliant idea. The news will report on medical emergencies, company turnarounds (as opposed to the positive management behaviour that might prevent a company from needing urgent action in the first place) and rescue missions in warzones, but not about the actions that prevent such disasters. Every day millions of heroic actions are taken – engineers design bridges strong enough not to collapse, pilots land at night and in the fog, mothers give their children the right medicine at the right time. All this is prevention. All this is very wise. All this is socially valuable. Yet none of it is visible to news journalists or consumers. My suggestion? There should be a Nobel Prize for prevention.

Unfortunately, journalists are prone to yet another misconception. They confuse 'absent' with 'unimportant'. Sometimes it's precisely what's absent – what hasn't happened – that is relevant. The absence of inflation, for example, although we've been expecting it for ten years. Or the absence of the collapse of the euro, even though it's been anticipated since 2010. Or the absence of a statistically likely worldwide pandemic. Journalists are innately blind to absences because they're so hyper-vigilant about what *is* happening. They miss the dogs that aren't barking yet – but might just one day bite.

17

NEWS KEEPS THE OPINION VOLCANO BUBBLING

What do you think about genetically modified wheat? In your opinion, do we need to legislate against artificial intelligence? What's your stance on self-driving cars? Are you in favour of legalising soft drugs?

As soon as we hear these or similar questions, our brains start generating opinions, even if we're no experts on the topic. The *opinion volcano* erupts of its own accord – it can't be controlled. This is a classic behavioural error: we form opinions on issues that don't really interest us, that cannot be fully answered, or that are too complex without in-depth analysis.

First, an example of something that doesn't really interest me. A few years ago I caught myself spouting opinions about a doping scandal, even though I didn't follow the sport involved and knew nothing about how the athletes had accomplished their performances. I could have spared myself these opinions and the resulting inner turmoil. I remember I stumbled across the topic when I happened to notice an article about it in the news. Without the news, my opinion volcano would have stayed peacefully dormant.

Second, an example of something fundamentally unknowable. Will the weather next summer be nice? In Switzerland there's a valley, a very remote valley, where there's a village called Muotathal. A few of its inhabitants – they call themselves the Muotathal Weather Forecasters – have made it their mission to predict the weather using things like ants and pine cones. Seriously. These oddballs aren't remotely embarrassed about it – they're highly adept at media interviews. Most of their predictions are wrong, of course, and the forecasters know that. They also know, however, that newspapers and TV stations love spotlighting them and asking them for their predictions, so they in turn keep making a three-act performance out of asking the ants. The fact is, nobody knows what the weather next summer will be like. Just because a minor opinion volcano is erupting in a mountain valley somewhere, doesn't mean you need to pay attention.

Third, an example of a question that's too complex for our brains. Will there be a world war in the next twenty years? It's impossible to say. As a consumer of the news, however, you're confronted almost daily with some story or other about the escalating tensions between China and the USA. Does that mean a clash between the two major powers is imminent? The only thing we can say for certain is that the likelihood is greater than zero and less than a hundred per cent. The intensity with which the media reports on geopolitical tensions has nothing to do with the actual probability of a world war.

And yet – especially with tough questions – we tend to come down very rapidly on one side or the other. Only then do we consult our brains for reasons to support our position. This is related to the *affect heuristic*. An affect is an instant, one-dimensional feeling. This feeling is superficial and comes in only two flavours: positive or negative, 'I like' or 'I don't like'. We see a face – *I like*. We hear about a murder – *I don't like*. Sun on the weekend – *I like*. Rain – *I don't like*. Affects have their place, but not when it comes to difficult questions, where we confuse them with a real answer. The news might as well be designed to generate unnecessary affects. In fact, it's pretty much impossible to consume the news affect-free – hence you're better off leaving it alone.

In short, it's a serious mistake to think we need to form an opinion about everything. Ninety per cent of our opinions are superfluous. Yet the news is constantly urging us to form opinions. This robs us of concentration and inner peace. Opinions are like noses – everybody has one. Consuming the news is like having a whole faceful of noses. Next time you're about to put your two pennyworth into a conversation on a popular topic, picture that. Or, to use a rather more civilised reference point, think of Marcus Aurelius, perhaps the greatest statesman of all time. He recommended exactly the same thing roughly two thousand years ago: 'You are at liberty *not* to form opinions about all and sundry, thereby sparing your soul unrest. For the things themselves demand no judgements from you.'

18

NEWS INHIBITS THOUGHT

Thought requires concentration, and concentration requires time without interruption. The moment you open yourself up to the torrent of news, your ability to concentrate will be swept away by the current. News will make a shallow thinker of you. Worse still, it will have a negative impact on your memory.

There are two types of memory. Long-term memory has a high storage capacity, while your working memory can only hold limited information (just try repeating a ten-digit phone number after only hearing it once). The path from working memory to long-term memory leads through a bottleneck in your brain. Anything you want to understand has to pass through this narrow passageway, and when it comes to abstract information, this takes concentration. News disrupts concentration, actively weakening your ability to understand things.

You wouldn't take a one-minute holiday to Paris. You wouldn't watch the latest blockbuster film in a three-minute compressed version of the best scenes. Why not? Because your brain needs time for new information to sink in. To build up concentration while you're reading, you need to give yourself at least ten minutes. Any less than that and your brain will process the information only superficially; it won't be able to store it. Ask yourself: what were the ten most important items in the news last month (that aren't still in the news today and are not sports-related news)? Most people can't even think of five. So why would you consume something that contributes nothing to your base of knowledge?

Online news is worse than print. One study conducted by Nicholas Carr revealed that our comprehension of a text decreases concomitantly with the number of hyperlinks it contains. Why? Because every time you come to a link, your brain has to decide whether or not to click on it. It's a constant distraction – as though someone were perpetually banging on your door or ringing your telephone every couple of seconds.

Online videos, however, are the biggest distraction of all, especially when they've got attention-grabbing thumbnails. Your brain struggles to muster the willpower not to click on them, wasting another few precious minutes. More than a few, probably, because straight away you'll be presented with another video. Then another. After a while you'll glance at the clock and wonder where the time went, and then you'll think, 'Where the hell was I in my work?'

Nobel Prize-winning economist Herbert Simon identified the problem nearly fifty years ago: 'What information consumes is rather obvious: it consumes the attention of its recipients. Hence a wealth of information creates a poverty of attention.' While in Simon's day we had to wait patiently for the news (for the clatter of the letterbox or the gong announcing the nightly television news) or go out of our way to find it (at the corner shop), the poverty of attention thanks to alerts, text messages, news feeds, news pop-ups and other interruptions has increased exponentially. We no longer have to find the news – the news finds us. Wherever we are.

Why do we abandon ourselves so thoughtlessly to digital distractions? Because media companies' algorithms know precisely what images and videos are best able to overcome our willpower. These algorithms are improving month by month, while your position, dear consumer of the news, is weakening in equal measure. Every news site you visit results in a battle between temptation and willpower – and in most cases temptation will get the upper hand. Why are you sending your brain into this unfair, bloody battle when there's nothing to be gained from it?

That's not even the worst of it. Not only do you have nothing to gain, but you have still more to lose. You will lose not only your concentration but also your willpower, which you could have used for something more sensible. The American psychology professor Roy Baumeister has shown that willpower functions rather like a muscle. You're not going to be bouncing around like a tennis ball after running a marathon. After extensive exercise, ATP (adenosine triphosphate) – which gives you energy in your muscles – gets depleted and must be recharged. It's the same for willpower. Baumeister talks about 'ego depletion': once your willpower is depleted, you don't have any left over for the next challenge. This is why workdays when you

77

consume a lot of news are so unsatisfying, even without the wasted time: you can barely get anything else done.

Since you will inevitably lose your battle with the news websites, the only rational strategy is to avoid the battlefield entirely: don't visit news websites. Why would you give these companies valuable minutes of your life, your urgently needed willpower and your personal data merely to get nonsense and advertising in return? Sounds like a pretty bad deal! The news is mental pollution. Keep your brain clean. It's your most important organ.

19

NEWS REWIRES OUR BRAINS

Your brain consists of roughly eighty-six billion nerve cells interconnected by more than a hundred trillion synapses. For a long time, scientists assumed that our brains were fully formed by the time we reached adulthood. Today we know that in fact our brains are constantly being reshaped, with nerve cells routinely breaking off old connections and creating new ones. To be more precise, the sensitivity of the receptors in the synapses changes. If we allow ourselves to be overwhelmed by a new cultural phenomenon such as the torrent of news, it reshapes our mental apparatus. It literally brainwashes us. This adaptation takes place on the level of biology. News rewires us. As a consequence, our brain works differently even when we're not actively reading the news. Differently, and – you've guessed it – not for the better. Researcher Nicholas Carr: 'When we go online, we enter an environment that promotes cursory reading, hurried and distracted thinking, and superficial learning. Even as the internet grants us easy access to vast amounts of information, it is turning us into shallower thinkers, literally changing the structure of our brain.'

Aspiring London cabbies are asked to cram an extraordinary amount of geographical information, called The Knowledge, into their heads in order to be given a taxi licence. London has 25,000 streets and countless sights. Taxi drivers have traditionally been expected to know every single one. No wonder their training takes three to four years – as long as it takes the brain to store a representative model of the capital.

Thanks to Google Maps and other mapping technologies, this laborious process will probably soon be obsolete. For now, however, researchers Eleanor Maguire, Katherine Woollett and Hugo Spiers at University College London have taken the opportunity to use these cab drivers in an experiment. They wondered whether the drivers' knowledge would be somehow observable in their brains. Did becoming a cabbie alter the brain's structure? They put the taxi drivers and a control group of bus drivers (who don't have to know the 25,000 streets, because they always drive the same routes) into an MRI scanner, repeating the process at intervals over several years. At first the researchers saw no difference. After the cabbies had got their licence, however, they observed a change in the structure of the hippocampus (important for long-term memory): the taxi drivers had significantly more nerve cells there than the bus drivers. Over the years, their biology diverged still further. Although the taxi drivers had a better mental street map, they were worse at noticing new geometric drawings. The bus drivers, however, had no difficulties. Progress in one area of the brain, it seemed, could only take place at the expense of regression elsewhere. Similar changes in brain structure have been observed in musicians, jugglers and people who grow up multilingual.

Similarly, researchers Kep-Kee Loh and Ryota Kanai of the University of Tokyo observed that the more frequently a person consumed different media at the same time, the fewer brain cells there were in the anterior cingulate cortex – the part of the brain responsible for attention, moral deliberation and impulse control, among other things. If you watch a news junkie, you'll see this in action: their concentration span shrinks and they have trouble controlling their emotions.

The more news you, dear reader, consume, the more you encourage the formation of neuronal circuits adapted to the flood of information and to multitasking. At the same time, the circuits necessary for absorbed reading and deep thought will atrophy. I always notice that the most passionate consumers of the news – even if they were once also passionate bookworms – no longer have the ability to read longer articles or books. After four or five pages they get tired, their attention dissipates, and they get restless. It's not because they're getting older or busier. Rather, the physical structure of their brain has changed. Michael Merzenich at the University of California in San Francisco puts it like this: 'We are training our brains to pay attention to the crap.'

You may think that you can cope with losing your capacity for concentrated reading. Deep reading, however, is demonstrably inseparable from clear thought. If you want to regain the skill of concentrating and immersing yourself in a subject, there's no option but to go news-free.

In my experience, your brain will need a year's abstinence from the news before it's capable of reading long texts without fatigue. The sooner you start, the sooner you'll regain your focus. And don't give up if it's hard at first. That's true of everything worthwhile.

20

NEWS PRODUCES FAKE FAME

A functioning society requires cooperation. A person's reputation is a signal: it tells us something about their potential as a collaborative partner. Unfortunately, in the world of the news, this signal is no longer reliable. In our evolutionary past, a person's reputation was directly related to their achievements or their power. If somebody caught a wild animal with their bare hands, saved another person's life or was skilled at making fires, they would be accorded a commensurate degree of respect (fame acquired through competence). A tribal leader who kept his position at the top of the clan by forming coalitions and playing a shrewd tactical game was also rewarded (fame acquired through power).

Later, long after we'd left the Stone Age behind us, there remained an indissoluble bond between fame and achievement or power. Aristotle, Sappho, Augustine, Beethoven, Newton, Darwin, Marie Curie, Einstein – all of them acquired fame by virtue of their competence. Emperors, kings and popes, meanwhile, acquired fame through power. Marcus Aurelius managed both – competence *and* power.

With the advent of the news, we suddenly found ourselves haunted by strange ghosts unknown to our ancestors: 'celebrities', people famous for reasons that are utterly irrelevant to society and our own lives. These days, the media bestows the rank of 'celebrity' upon talk-show hosts, sports commentators, supermodels and pop stars for such trivial reasons that it undermines the relationship between fame and achievement, creating *fake fame*. Celebrity is a self-referential system. A celebrity is a celebrity because they're a celebrity. How they became a celebrity is soon forgotten and plays no role in the media circus. Journalists report on the celebrity because they're a celebrity. It's virtually impossible to name someone who became famous before the advent of the news media whose fame wasn't based on competence or power. At most, you could come up with a few criminals.

Ever heard of Donald Henderson? He led the World Health Organization team that wiped out smallpox. For thousands of years, smallpox was considered one of the world's most dangerous diseases, both highly infectious and highly likely to be fatal. Henderson's systematic immunisation programme combatting the disease finally achieved the supposedly impossible: smallpox was defeated. For good. This is the only time a deadly pathogen has been completely exterminated – one of the greatest triumphs in the history of medicine. Henderson was showered with accolades. In 1986 he was awarded the National Medal of Science, and in 2002 he received the Presidential Medal of Freedom – the USA's highest honour. Nor did Henderson shy away from the media. On the contrary. After smallpox was eliminated, he became a dean at Johns Hopkins University – one of the most important medical universities in the world – and a senior advisor to the US government. Yet his name appeared hardly anywhere in the media. Why?

Because the media focuses on celebrities. Henderson 'only' had his achievement to offer – no weird hairdo, no gobby opinions, no smart designer clothes. Thanks to this – and since dealing with a subject like infectious disease is too strenuous – he held no interest for the media.

Now, celebrity isn't bad *per se*. What is unfortunate, however, is that in the media's eyes celebrities crowd out all the people who have actually achieved something. The more celebrities are plastered across the pages of news-papers, on TV programmes, blogs and in tweets, the less room there is for people like Henderson.

The news media has severed the bond between fame and accomplishment. If you consume the news, you won't merely lose the battle with fake news – you'll lose the battle with fake fame, too. Don't do that to yourself. And don't do it to society.

21

NEWS MAKES US SMALLER THAN WE REALLY ARE

As a writer, I know precisely where I stand at each moment in the hierarchy of authors. There are the weekly bestseller lists. There are readers awarding stars out of five on dozens of websites. There is a pyramid of literary prizes, including longlists and shortlists. There is the ever-fluctuating sales ranking on Amazon. There are online reviews – hymns of praise and hatchet jobs. There are likes and followers on social media. Second by second, I can track my status as a writer with complete precision. If I can't handle this hyper-comparativeness, I'm in the wrong profession.

Writers are perhaps an extreme example of the transparency of hierarchies. But there's a problem here: every working person operates within a hierarchy. Architects, developers, insurance agents, bankers, chefs. Most of us are extremely sensitive to changes in status. Why?

As human beings we're one of roughly four thousand species of mammal. This has profound consequences for our psychology. We're hugely invested in our offspring. Carrying a child is draining. After birth, most mammals cannot survive without protection, food and instruction. The mother is unable to mate with potentially better partners during pregnancy and nursing: a significant opportunity cost. Female mammals are thus extremely choosy when it comes to mating. Access to resources is their key criterion. And because higher status equates to better access to resources among all mammals, *Homo sapiens* included, women – and I'm over-simplifying here, of course – tend to choose higher-status men. This happens largely subconsciously. 'Falling in love' is the mechanism evolution has designed to accomplish it.

The counterpart to the female's preference for high status is the male's latent anxiety around its lack. And because women get half their genes from their father, this drive to attain status is rooted in them too. Women also have their own status pyramid.

The upshot? We all arrange ourselves in hierarchies. In the workplace, the military, the church, sports, our neigh-bourhood, even in the playground. We can't escape them. Now you may be thinking: so what?

Changes in status aren't purely a matter of emotion. Sir Michael Marmot, a professor at University College London, has shown that people with low status fall ill more quickly, suffer more frequently from depression and die earlier. Status has significant physical consequences.

What does all this have to do with the news? Quite simply, news makes the already rather brutal natural hier-archy even more brutal by reporting disproportionately on the beautiful and successful. It functions like a magnifying glass. The publication of the annual rich lists (the Forbes Global 2000 in the USA, while other countries have their own versions) isn't a happy day for a 'normal' millionaire, let alone for us non-millionaires. Our ridiculous obsession with 'Manager of the Year', 'Businessperson of the Year', 'Athlete of the Year', 'Publicist of the Year', 'Artist of the Year', 'Pop Singer of the Year', 'Gardener of the Year' sends a subconscious signal to every 'normal' manager, businessperson, athlete and so on that floods their bodies with harmful stress hormones. The procession of beautiful young models in billboard advertising is a stab to the heart of every 'normal' man and woman – with all the negative consequences, including physical ones.

Yet the media also reports on the other extreme of the bell curve – the hard-luck stories, the losers, the hideously ugly, the psychopaths, the failures. Does that make us 'normal' people secretly jubilant? No, because the rule in psychology is that bad counts for twice as much as good. Although comparing ourselves to someone on the fringes makes us feel good about our status, comparing ourselves to a Bill Gates or a Charlize Theron makes us feel twice as bad. The net effect of the media coverage on our internal sense of equilibrium is therefore negative.

In short, consuming the news widens the pool of potential competitors to include the entire world. We compare ourselves to people who have absolutely nothing whatsoever to do with us. As a result we feel smaller than we really are. Of course, this could be rationally countered – but we don't do that. The emotional consequences are real, bringing physical and hormonal changes in their wake. Our stress level rises. Our serotonin level falls. We bow our heads and shuffle our feet, broken. We make life harder for ourselves than it already is. High time to opt out – out of our absurd consumption of the news media and our absurd race to achieve status.

22

NEWS MAKES US PASSIVE

News stories are predominantly concerned with things you cannot change. Terrorists have detonated a bomb somewhere, a volcano is erupting in Iceland, a famine in the Sahara has killed a hundred thousand people, an American president has tweeted something absurd, immigrants are pouring over the border, Apple has removed the headphone jack from its new models, Volkswagen has failed emissions tests, Brad Pitt is divorcing Angelina Jolie, and on and on and on. None of this is within your control. Hardly anything you hear on the news will be something you can change.

The daily litany of things we cannot change makes us passive. The news wears us down until we're miserable, hopeless pessimists. Of course we want to help. Of course we want to intervene and make the world a slightly better place. But our time is already at its limit. How are we supposed to stop a volcano erupting on the other side of the planet, avert a terrorist attack or save people from starvation? We're cursed to watch these disasters unfold while knowing that there's nothing we can do to prevent them.

When our brains encounter information without us having the possibility of acting on it, we gradually assume the role of a victim. Our impulse to take action fades. We become passive. The scientific term for this is *learned helplessness*.

American psychologists Martin Seligman and Steven Maier identified learned helplessness in the 1960s, initially through experiments on animals. They attached an electrode to rats' tails, then delivered electric shocks that were not painful but annoying. The first group of rats could turn a wheel and switch off the shocks. These rats had control over their situation. In the second group, however, turning the wheel had no effect. These rats were at the mercy of their fate.

Although both groups had the same input (electrical shocks of the same severity and frequency), their behaviour after the series of shocks was completely different. The rats in the first group displayed no unusual behaviour. They went on their way as though nothing had happened. The animals in the second group, however, underwent a significant shift in personality. They became shy, passive, and had a reduced sex drive. They showed signs of anhedonia (a reduced capacity to feel joy), an aversion to new things and a fear of ambiguity.

The news might as well have a similar effect on human beings as the electric shocks did on the rats in the second group. Stories and images in the news whip us up emotionally, but we have no wheel to turn and change the reported facts. The smartest thing, of course, would be to cut off the supply entirely, but most of us find it too difficult.

Most insidious of all is that learned helplessness doesn't just make us passive about what's on the news. Nope.

Learned helplessness spills over into every area of our lives. Once the news has made us passive, we tend to behave passively towards our family and our jobs as well – precisely where we *do* have room for manoeuvre.

British media researcher Jodie Jackson takes a similar view: 'When we tune into the news, we are constantly confronted with unresolved problems and the narrative does not inspire much hope that they will ever be solved.' It's no surprise, then, that we feel depressed when we consume the news, which confronts us with problems that are mostly impossible to solve. Two thousand years ago, the great philosopher Epictetus began his *Enchiridion* with the following sentence: 'Some things are in our control and others not.' The gist? It's idiotic to dwell on things that we cannot control. Nearly everything we hear on the news is outside our sphere of influence. So you can safely disregard it.

Devote your energies to things you can influence. There are more than enough of those – but an earthquake on the other side of the planet isn't one of them.

23

NEWS IS INVENTED
BY JOURNALISTS

Good journalists take time over their articles. They check facts, make an effort to depict the complexity of a situation, and think deeply about the issue at hand. As in every profession, however, there are also incompetent hacks who lack the drive or the talent to achieve anything worthwhile. Or – and perhaps this is most common – the time. As a consumer of the media you can't tell which one they're missing, but the result is the same regardless.

Many of them have no skin in the game – they're risking nothing. If journalists write crap, it almost never comes back to bite them. Maybe the odd angry letter from a reader. If they make a serious mistake, they might be hauled over the coals by their editor-in-chief. Most likely, however, nothing will happen at all. The article will simply be swept away by the next piece of breaking news. Not so for business people or investors. An investor who makes a bad decision will feel the impact straight away in their bank balance. An entrepreneur whose strategy flops will have to face the music.

That said, bad journalism is not solely the fault of bad journalists. The problem is that these mostly brilliant people have become accidentally trapped in an industry that makes less and less sense. Juggling the news has become mindless. Many of these clever writers don't have the time to do investigative work or in-depth research. More importantly, they don't have the time to think or the space or opportunity to explain complicated ideas. Pressure on journalists has risen exponentially since the turn of the century. Many media companies require their journalists to produce up to a dozen stories a day – all in pursuit of clicks and likes. Maintaining high standards is impossible.

It's extremely difficult to write something thought-provoking about a single topic, let alone on ten different ones over the course of just one day. Yet this is precisely the 'mission impossible' demanded of journalists. Generally, unless the media is funded by taxpayers, like the BBC, employing specialists is far too expensive, so everything necessarily remains superficial.

Consumers, deafened by the endless din of the news, rarely notice this. Journalists are only too aware of it. The fear of being unmasked as a charlatan is omnipresent in the industry. Journalists suffer as a result, becoming depressed or cynical, or both at once. No wonder most of them switch sides after a few years and take a job in corporate communications – less stress, better pay, regular hours. They're no longer trying to save the world.

In 2015 the job site CareerCast surveyed 200 jobs in the USA, asking about workplace environment, stress, salary and future prospects. Which profession ended up languishing in last place? Newspaper journalist – ranking even lower than forest ranger and soldier.

We can't really accuse media companies of having screwed up journalism – it was the internet giants who stole their advertising revenue, undermining how they do business: Google, Facebook and Amazon. Yet these giants are only as successful as we consumers make them by spending our time on their platforms. Holding journalists responsible for the current mess is like holding sugar cubes responsible for our poor diet. Our own behaviour as consumers has led to a race to the bottom. The only way to avoid losing the race is not to take part. This is my recommendation to you as a reader – and especially to my journalist friends. All self-respecting journalists should steer clear of news journalism, just as no chef who takes pride in his work would start a career at McDonald's.

24

NEWS IS MANIPULATIVE

Our evolutionary past has equipped us with a powerful ability to sniff out nonsense, bluffing and lies in face-to-face communication. Subconsciously we recognise the signs of manipulation, signs that go beyond the verbal: gestures, facial expressions and indications of anxiety such as trembling hands, blushing and body odour. When we still lived in small groups, we nearly always knew the messenger's background. Information came with a halo of meta-information. Even in the Middle Ages, most messages were delivered orally. You knew the messenger and were thus well placed to judge whether to believe the message.

These days it's much harder to distinguish between truthful, unbiased news items and those with an ulterior motive. There's a vast industry of lobbying and leverage at work behind the scenes. 'For every reporter in the United States, there are more than four public relations specialists working hard to get them to write what their bosses want them to say,' media entrepreneur Clay A. Johnson has remarked. Worldwide, the public relations industry generates a turnover of between fifteen and thirty billion dollars a year – the best evidence that journalists and consumers can be successfully manipulated, influenced or won over to a cause. Companies, interest groups and other organisations wouldn't pay such dizzying sums to publicists if they got no return on their investment. If PR advisors can manipulate journalists – people who are professionally required to be sceptical about powerful organisations – then what chance do we have of avoiding their subtle influence?

Let's take the story about a nurse called Nayirah. She was a fifteen-year-old Kuwaiti girl who testified before the US Congress prior to the Gulf War in 1991. She claimed to have seen Iraqi soldiers murdering babies in her hospital in Kuwait. Virtually every media outlet reported on her testimony. The American public was outraged, and the story helped swing the vote in favour of the war. Nayirah's testimony, which at the time was taken at face value, later proved to be part of an extensive propaganda campaign run on behalf of the Kuwaiti government.

Today we would call Nayirah's story a classic example of fake news. Propaganda is nothing new. Ever since the advent of the printing press and the sudden multitude of flyers in its wake, people have been grappling with fake news. A hundred years ago, the American writer Upton Sinclair wrote, 'When you read your daily paper, are you reading facts or propaganda?'

These days, however, two things are new. First, the sheer volume of fake news has mushroomed. At least it costs something to print a flyer. Publishing digital fake news costs almost nothing. Second, today's fake news is specifically targeted at individual consumers, known as micro-targeting, and thus packs more of a punch.

Soon we won't even need human beings to produce fake news. Intelligent computer programs can already write it by themselves. In the future, these automatically generated articles will be perfectly tailored to the preferences of the consumer. Resisting will be near impossible, even for the critical. Whether these articles have anything in common with the truth is secondary – the main thing is that they generate clicks and thereby advertising revenue. Or they sway our opinion or encourage us to buy something.

Of course, we're not just talking about texts, articles, posts and tweets. Today's hyper-intelligent computers can already create images and video clips. For the time being a practised eye can spot them – for instance, if utterly different words are put into the mouth of a particular president, complete with the perfect voice, expressions and gestures. Yet within a few years, only artificial intelligence will be able to tell which news items have been generated by computers and which have not.

In the quagmire that is the world of the news, new articles are springing up like mushrooms – some edible, some poisonous. Telling the difference between ones that are true and ones that are lies will only become more baffling. Moreover, even established news organisations are increasingly featuring 'advertorials' and 'native advertising': paid-for puff pieces camouflaged as editorials. Studies suggest that we have already passed 'the Inversion', meaning that more than fifty per cent of the content, users and clicks on the internet are fake. If you want to protect yourself as much as possible against manipulation, it's best to keep well clear of the news. A pleasant side effect? You'll be rid of a huge bulk of crap advertising. The news nearly always has some sort of advertising in tow, and at base it's pure manipulation. Adverts are trying to flog us products we don't need or can't afford – otherwise we'd buy them without advertising. Adverts are as superfluous as news. Ditch it.

25

NEWS KILLS CREATIVITY

Pseudo-knowledge stifles our creativity. This is one of the reasons why mathematicians, writers, composers and entrepreneurs usually pull off their most creative accomplishments when they're young. Their minds are free to roam through wide, uninhabited space, encouraging them to develop and pursue novel ideas.

I don't know a single creative person who is also a news junkie – no authors, no composers, no mathematicians, no physicists, no scientists, no musicians, no designers, no architects and no painters. On the other hand, I know plenty of extremely uncreative people who consume vast quantities of news.

Why is this? No matter the question, problem or task, your first idea is usually one you've heard somewhere before. Initial ideas are rarely creative. So before I read a book or a long article, I take a few minutes and force myself to come up with my own ideas about the issue under discussion. It's laborious but valuable, because I know that as soon as I start reading, the author's thoughts will fill my brain, and I'll have little chance of forming my own. If I gradually immerse myself in the book after having done some of my own reflection, however, then I can compare the author's ideas to my own. Sometimes they coincide; sometimes not. It doesn't matter. What's crucial is that the reading experience becomes a sort of mental dialogue with the author. This tactic is highly effective with books and long articles, but not with the news. The news is specifically constructed so that you *cannot* form your own thoughts. You're overwhelmed before you can even get off the starting blocks. The news is brief, garish, fast-paced and extremely oversimplified – ideal fodder for thoughtless consumption.

The creativity-stifling effect of the news may also have something to do with a simple factor we have already discussed: concentration. Creativity requires concentration. If you're constantly distracted by the news, you can't form new ideas. To 'give birth to a dancing star' as Friedrich Nietzsche once phrased it, you need a bit of peace and quiet on the maternity ward.

One objection I often hear is that if we only consume information that matches our circle of competence and disregard everything else, then we're ruling out any chance of a serendipitous discovery. Yet the power of serendipity is overrated. Hand on heart, how often have you stumbled across information from a completely different area that has strengthened your circle of competence? Almost never. Of course, you can be open to insights from all angles. And sometimes you really can draw creative ideas from other fields. But time you spend grazing in fields unrelated to your area of expertise is time you can't spend systematically tilling the soil of your own circle of competence. There are only twenty-four hours in the day, after all.

My recommendation? If you really want to go fishing in a different pond, set aside half a day per month and go to a large bookshop. Flick through the new publications from as many areas as possible. And yes, buy a few of them. But don't spend every day surfing random news sites in the hopes of stumbling across a creative idea that will catapult your career to greater heights. If that's how you manage your time, you're in for one long nosedive. Another tip from my own practice: I schedule regular meetings with experts in other fields. I need to have lunch anyway, why not with masters of their craft, with scientists and experts in matters I know little about? I can also pass on information from the world of writing, which may enrich them in return. More on this in Chapter 33.

News junkies sometimes justify their behaviour by claiming that the news gives them a fresh perspective. Yet if we take an objective look at the stream of news, we can see that it's always the same. A scandal here, a bomb there, an actor here, a central bank chairman there, athletes breaking records, companies holding press conferences, industries growing, others shrinking, the stock market dancing up and down, some group of people somewhere are outraged, and the occasional plane falls from the sky. 'Slowly you realise. Nothing new,' wrote playwright Max Frisch about the media. An eternal diagnosis.

There's another accusation I occasionally hear, too: not only do you miss out when you abstain strictly from the news, but you stay a 'nerd' all your life. This is true, but remember that 'nerd' is another word for 'master'. True value – for ourselves and for society – is generated solely within our circle of competence. It cannot be any other way. Someone who is the best in their niche has achieved mastery. Someone who has dipped a toe into hundreds of different topics and drooled over every titbit of news won't suddenly turn into a creative genius. They may not be a nerd (although this is actually a compliment), but they'll always be a bog-standard idiot.

26

NEWS ENCOURAGES CRAP: STURGEON'S LAW

Theodore Sturgeon was one of the most prolific American science-fiction writers of the 1950s and 1960s. Yet with success came malice. Sturgeon was the subject of endless condescension from literary critics, who jeered that ninety per cent of all sci-fi was rubbish. Sturgeon reacted coolly. His response? Yeah, that's true. Ninety per cent of *everything* that's published is rubbish, regardless of genre. His answer has gone down in history as Sturgeon's Law.

The American philosopher Daniel Dennett later broadened Sturgeon's Law to include everything. It's not just ninety percent of all literature that's crap but ninety percent of everything – scientific studies, operas, start-ups, shirt buttons, PowerPoint presentations, dog food brands. Sturgeon's Law applies to the news, too. Take a moment to think about how much of what's reported in the news doesn't actually deserve a second of your time – the derogatory, the abstruse, the coarse, the silly, the ridiculous. A person who ate a hundred hot dogs in fifteen minutes and was rushed to hospital to get his stomach pumped. A person who drove his car into a river to save money on a car wash – and drowned. A woman who smeared toothpaste on her breasts in an attempt to make them bigger. A man who poisoned his dog because it chewed up his briefcase. These are real-life examples.

Sturgeon's Law is worse than the general irrelevance of the news. Irrelevance means that consuming the news won't lead you to make better decisions, either in your private or professional life. Usually it has the opposite effect. Sturgeon's Law, however, means that newspapers, broadcasters and websites are increasingly turning into a sort of large-scale bathroom wall.

You'd expect the media to function as a bullshit filter for readers, listeners and viewers. Yet increasingly the news media is trending towards the opposite, becoming a magnet for bullshit of all kinds. Nonsense is not only tolerated and repeated, it's actively given top billing. The people producing this kind of rubbish know only too well that the media will lap it up, thereby encouraging other people to produce even more of it. 'Every man should have a built-in automatic crap detector operating inside him,' wrote novelist Ernest Hemingway fifty years ago.

Still, this shouldn't stop you building your own automatic crap detector. Be aware that not all media outlets publish rubbish. There are quality publications which contain things that are irrelevant but rarely derogatory or silly. Yet there are an increasing number of media outlets – especially free newspapers and online – whose business model involves shovelling the greatest possible magnitude of rubbish over the greatest possible area. Not because the owners of these companies prefer juvenile comedy. Or because the editors are primitive goons. On the contrary.

The companies and editors know exactly what they're doing: they publish crap because their consumers lap it up. By publishing crap, the media encourages crap.

Sturgeon's Law applies not merely to content but also to the way in which it's reported. The mixture of facts, claims, product placement and opinions is an unappetising cocktail you'd be better off pouring down the sink, even if the news *is* dealing with something serious.

Since you've bought this book, I'm going to assume we're largely in agreement. One word of advice, however: don't try to purge the world of nonsense. You won't succeed. The world can stay irrational longer than you can stay insane. If you bear Sturgeon's Law in mind and stoically accept it, you'll have a better life.

27

NEWS GIVES US THE
ILLUSION OF EMPATHY

The news lulls us into a warm, all-inclusive sense of common humanity. We're all citizens of the world. We're all subject to the same troubles. We're all connected. The planet is a global village. We sing 'We Are the World' while swaying back and forth in harmony with thousands of others, holding our tiny lighters. This sense of empathy, magnified a thousand-fold, feels wonderfully soft and cosy – yet it achieves absolutely nothing. This magical sense of all-encompassing, worldwide fellowship is a gigantic act of self-deceit. The fact is, consuming the news does not connect us to other people and cultures. We're connected to each other because we cooperate, trade, cultivate friendships and relationships, fall in love.

Whenever I tell people I've stopped reading the news, I'm always accused of taking no interest in the plight of impoverished people, or in wars or atrocities.

My response is as follows: but should I? I'm sure there are bad things happening on other continents or even other planets. Should I also 'take an interest' in that? Where do we draw the line? Tellingly, the media will report exhaustively on a light-aircraft crash in which a few people from the publication's own country died, but hardly at all on a comparable crash affecting a hundred times more people from, say, Kamchatka.

Besides, 'taking an interest by consuming media' – could anybody be more self-deluded? Genuine concern entails action. Wallowing in your own empathy by watching earthquake victims crawling out of rubble on TV isn't simply not helpful, it's actually repulsive. If you really care about the fate of earthquake victims, war refugees or famine victims, give money. Not attention. Not work. Not prayers. Money.

By following, say, the fate of earthquake victims on a news website, you're actually giving your attention to the people running the platform, not the victims themselves. Your attention won't make a blind bit of difference to the victims, but it certainly will to the platforms. Doubly so, in fact: first, because they make money by selling your attention to advertisers; second, because it enables them to gather more of your personal data – your user behaviour, your personality and your emotional weaknesses – and use it to bombard you with increasingly targeted advertisements. Your attention helps the news media, not the victims. And you're harming yourself.

Indeed, contributing your own manpower to a cause is of limited to zero use. Don't go to the Sahara to build a water pump with your own two hands. This well-intentioned lunacy is known as *volunteer's folly*. You might manage to build one well per day, but if you do a day's work at your regular job (working within your circle of competence) and send the money you earn to Africa, you can help build a hundred wells a day. That's of far more use to the world's poor. Don't donate your manpower on site; donate money from where you already are.

If you stop reading the news, you'll have reclaimed a whole month out of the year. Translate part of this time into money (perhaps in the form of overtime or by taking on a side job) and donate what you earn.

One objection I hear a lot is this: 'If you don't consume the news, you don't know where help is most urgently needed.' This, too, is a cognitive error. The news media is biased about what disasters it covers. It reports on disasters that are a) new, b) visually striking and c) can be told through the lens of individual human stories. The conflict in Palestine is getting boring after all these years, viruses aren't very photogenic, and thawing permafrost only gets exciting if a car gets stuck in it. These three criteria have nothing to do with an objective assessment of global suffering. Slow developments towards potential disasters – which may still be preventable – hardly ever make the news.

Let me assure you, your humanity is not measured according to how much misery you consume on the news. Nor by the sympathy it elicits. My tip? Assume that there's enough suffering in the world even without the news. Make regular donations to established aid organisations. They – not the media – have the best sense of where help is most needed.

28

NEWS ENCOURAGES
TERRORISM

Gersau is a village in the middle of Switzerland, idyllically situated on Lake Lucerne: a tiny, picturesque place with two thousand inhabitants. The microclimate in this 'Riviera on Lake Lucerne' (according to the tourist brochures) is so mild they even have a few palm trees – a rarity north of the Alps. For centuries Gersau was an independent republic. The village wanted no part in the Swiss Federation, and for three hundred years it was given free rein. Only when Napoleon invaded Switzerland in 1798 was its independence revoked. When the French troops withdrew, the village re-declared independence – but this only lasted four years. Today, Gersau is part of Switzerland.

Let's try a thought experiment. Imagine you're a Gersau villager, and you want to regain independence. You feel obliged by the long historic tradition of independence. Maybe, you feel that you've been unjustly treated by the rest of Switzerland. What options do you have to make people listen to your demands? You could gather like-minded compatriots and pass a resolution at a community meeting. But nobody would take you seriously. Certainly not outside the village. You could write a blog – which would never be read. You could employ a PR firm, but that, too, would come to nothing. Or you could set off a bomb outside parliament in Bern. With a giant placard in the background – 'Free Gersau!' – you would capture national and international attention within minutes. Of course, everybody would condemn your behaviour in the strongest terms, but . . . you would spark a debate.

Now imagine the press did not exist. What then? The bomb explodes. Windows shatter. Passers-by are injured. The attack is discussed at the market and down the pub. Outside Bern, however, interest would fizzle. Next day the square outside parliament would look the same as before, and you'd have accomplished nothing.

Terrorism only works thanks to the news media. The terrorists' true weapon isn't the bomb but the fear triggered by the bomb. The actual threat is relatively small, but the perceived threat is immense. This balancing act is made possible by the news media.

Since 2001, terrorists have killed on average fifty people per year within the EU. By comparison, 80,000 EU citizens die each year in traffic accidents and 60,000 by suicide. In Germany, the numbers are as follows: fewer than three people per year die at the hands of terrorists, compared to 3,000 road deaths and 10,000 suicides. The risk of being killed by a terrorist is astronomically smaller than the risk of being killed by your own hand. Paradoxically, the news makes it seem like it's the other way around.

A terrorist's primary goal isn't to kill people. Their goals are strategic: they're seeking political change; they're supporting separatist movements; they're trying to discredit the ruling party. Above all, they want people to pay attention to their demands – attention they receive in the form of news and the ensuing backlash.

For political scientist Martha Crenshaw at Stanford University, terrorists are entirely rational actors. 'Terrorism is a logical choice . . . when the power ratio of government to challenger is high.' In other words, terrorists themselves are powerless. The only halfway promising method of forcing political change is to sow fear and chaos. And for that they need the news media.

There's a reason why terrorism was unknown in the Middle Ages or the Roman Empire: in those days there was no news media. Of course, attacks, acts of sabotage and murder happened before the advent of journalism, but the perpetrators were trying to inflict concrete, specific damage – not to manipulate feeling and opinion.

The Israeli historian Yuval Noah Harari has remarked, 'Terrorists are masters of mind control. They kill very few people but nevertheless manage to terrify billions and rattle huge political structures such as the European Union or the United States.' As he has also noted, 'The theatre of terror cannot succeed without publicity. Unfortunately, the media all too often provides this publicity for free. It obsessively reports terror attacks and greatly inflates their danger, because reports on terrorism sell newspapers much better than reports on diabetes or air pollution.'

If we all adhered strictly to a news-free diet, the phenomenon of terrorism would dissipate as quickly as the smoke after an attack. If you consume the news, just be aware that you're unintentionally supporting terrorism. It's up to you to pull the handbrake.

29

NEWS DESTROYS OUR
PEACE OF MIND

What constitutes a good life? To put it another way: how should you live your life so that you can one day look back on it as 'successful' and 'good'? Until you can answer this fundamental question, your life will be a non-stop crisis-coping machine. Without a clear philosophy here, you risk life passing you by.

It doesn't matter so much what philosophy you choose. The main thing is to think it through properly and make a choice. I set out mine in my book *The Art of the Good Life*. Your goals may be similar to mine. They may be quite different. It's not important – what *is* important is that you've got goals, and you're clear about what they are.

If we survey the last 2,500 years – since philosophers first began to write their ideas down – we find a remarkable degree of overlap between philosophers. 'Inner peace' was nearly always considered a key component of a successful life, though in the old days this concept was often expressed in terms of 'tranquillity', 'equanimity', an 'inner strong-hold', 'serenity' or 'peace of mind'. Peace of mind arises in part through the absence of toxic emotions. The faster you can eliminate toxic emotions like envy, anger and self-pity from your emotional repertoire, the better.

What has this got to do with the news? Quite simply, the news is wreaking havoc on your peace of mind. It's not just the frantic sense of chaos but the permanently negative emotions it's always stirring up. Fear, annoyance, jealousy, anger and self-pity are predominately triggered these days by the news. You only have to read the comments underneath any online article. The hatred you find there is alarming, especially when you bear in mind that the website's algorithms have already filtered out the nastiest ones automatically. News and comments about the news bring out the worst in humanity. Keep an airtight seal between yourself and this incubator of negativity, abandoning the hopelessly infected to the virus.

What is wisdom? Think of a wise man or a wise woman – your personal ideal, a beacon of humanity. Someone like Socrates, Confucius, the Buddha, Jesus, Marcus Aurelius, Hildegard of Bingen, Mother Teresa, Martin Luther King, Gandhi or any of the 'wise women' in the biblical texts. Now imagine this person alive today. Your image of them would be completely ruined if they were constantly checking the news on their smartphone. News cannot answer the Big Questions. In fact, it suggests these questions don't exist at all. Virtually any type of content – novels, nonfiction books, films, music, visual art, academic research, essays – is a better conduit for wisdom than the news. Wisdom and news consumption simply aren't a good fit.

A cornerstone of any sensible life philosophy is as follows: there are things you can control and there are things you can't control, and it's idiotic to trouble yourself about things you can't control. The Stoics, a very practical school of philosophy in Ancient Greece and Rome, symbolised their belief system with the image of an archer. An archer can control which bow he chooses, which arrow he selects from his quiver, how far back he draws the bow and how still he holds it. But from the moment he lets the arrow fly, it's beyond his control. A gust of wind may knock the arrow off course. Or it may break mid-flight. Or something might get between the flying arrow and its target. Or the target may move.

Nintey-nine point nine per cent of all world events are outside your control. You have no influence on what's happening in the world, where or how. It's much more sensible to focus your energies on things you *can* control. Granted, this will be a much smaller world than the planet as a whole. But that's just the way it is. You can influence what happens in your life, your family, your neighbourhood, your city, your job, but the rest you simply have to accept.

The philosopher Epictetus offered another important argument two thousand years ago: 'You become what you give your attention to . . . If you yourself don't choose what thoughts and images you expose yourself to, someone else will.' If you consume the news, you're becoming another person, another character – a worse one than if you filled your mind with wise content. To achieve wisdom, we should choose 'a limited number of master thinkers and digest their works,' suggested the philosopher Seneca (also two thousand years ago). Consuming the news is like a frantic, never-ending journey. 'When a person spends all his time in foreign travel,' noted Seneca, 'he ends by having many acquaintances, but no friends.'

The freedom to choose for ourselves what's relevant is fundamental to a good life. More fundamental even than the freedom to express our opinions. An individual has the right not to be sent crazy by things that are clamorously pretending to be new and important. Our brains are full. We've got to cleanse them, detoxify them, free them of junk – not continually chuck in more. Reduction is far more beneficial than addition. Less is the new more.

30

NOT CONVINCED?

Over the previous pages you've been presented with a whole arsenal of arguments against consuming the news. I hope by now you're convinced of the benefits. You only need to read this chapter if you're not. If that's the case, please give me one more chance. I have a suggestion for you that will only take twenty minutes – a mere blip in comparison to the time I hope you'll save afterwards.

Take a piece of paper, put it on the table and divide it up into ten columns. Number the columns from left to right with the last ten years – 2011, 2012, 2013 to 2020, for example. Draw a horizontal line through the middle of the paper, splitting each column into two halves. In the upper half, note down the most important news reports you can recall from that year. Please don't cheat or resort to Google. The point of this exercise is to show you how fleeting the news is. So, for instance, under 2016 you could write, 'Trump elected president of America'. Under 2012, 'War begins in Syria'. And so forth. You'll find that of the 200,000 news reports you've stuffed into your brain over the past ten years, virtually nothing has been retained.

In the bottom half of the column, write down the major developments in your own life: triumphs, challenges, epiphanies, big changes in your personality, your family, your career, your circle of friends, your free time, your psychological and spiritual life. Perhaps you got married. Perhaps you had a baby. Perhaps you decided to embark upon a course of study. Perhaps you were fired. Perhaps you got cancer, or your father died. Perhaps you won the lottery, bought a house, travelled round the world, founded a start-up. Whatever.

Next, consider whether the news reports (top of the page) directly influenced the developments in your life (bottom of the page). Maybe the refugee crisis in 2015 led you to give up your job a year later and launch your own aid project. If so, take a pen and draw a thick connecting line between the refugee crisis in 2015 and your aid project in 2016. How many connecting lines do you end up with over the course of ten years?

Wait, you didn't draw a single line? Don't be surprised. That's normal. The world of the news and the world of your own life are two completely different universes; they have nothing to do with each other. This means you can safely ignore the whole circus, lock, stock and barrel. Even if you did find a line, I doubt you needed the news as a transmission mechanism. Let's say you lost your mother-in-law in the Germanwings plane crash of 2015; this connection still had nothing to do with the news report itself.

Still not convinced? Wow, you're a tough nut to crack! Okay, one more suggestion: spend a whole day in your city library, skimming through old newspapers – ones that are ten or twenty years old. You'll find that nearly all the articles miss the important topics. The journalists didn't merely fail to recognise the signs of the times, they picked the wrong signs then misinterpreted them. Flick through a paper from the year 2007, for instance, and you'll find virtually no reference to the impending financial crisis. At most there'll be some gushing puff piece about a hyper-successful trader, washed down with a heady mixture of trivial stories, factoids and vapid scandals whose protagonists are nobodies today. Most likely it will all seem quite ridiculous — as ridiculous as today's 'breaking news' will seem to you in ten years' time.

The archives of the reputable Swiss current affairs TV programme *Tagesschau* are available online. Why don't we take a peek? This book was published in Germany on 2 September 2019. What was happening precisely twenty-five years ago? Let's google 'Tagesschau 2.9.1994'. What do we find? The conservative-leaning Christian Social Union had a party conference. Construction workers were protesting cuts to the extra compensation they received for working during bad weather conditions. Gorbachev (then no longer in office) spoke out in favour of land reform in East Germany. The last few Russian soldiers stationed in Germany withdrew. The Belgians were celebrating the fiftieth anniversary of the liberation. Chancellor Kohl presided over the official opening of a museum. China and Russia wanted to foster more collaboration. Volkswagen wanted to expand into India. The football club Werder Bremen was top of the league. A children's festival in Potsdam. The lottery numbers. Imagine what would have happened if

Tagesschau had been unable to air for some reason. The consequences? Precisely none. The news industry is society's appendix – permanently inflamed and completely pointless. You're better off simply having it removed.

31

WHAT ABOUT
DEMOCRACY?: PART 1

Perhaps I've managed to shake your faith in the news a little bit. I hope I've been able to convince you and a few other readers that a news-free life is a better life. One thing, however, is clear: the vast majority of people are convinced that a daily scan of worldwide current events is part of an educated, engaged life. Giving up the news is quickly painted as immoral, just as in medieval times it was considered immoral not to attend church on Sundays. The question of democracy – isn't the news an essential part of it? – is the most common objection in this regard. Luckily, it's also easy to refute.

Let's assume we all stopped reading the news. Would we harm democracy by doing so? Well, let's break down the question into two parts. How can citizens make good choices at elections and referendums? And: who keeps an eye on those in power?

I'll start by addressing the first question. Can we give up the news and still cast sensible votes? Is political discourse even possible without the news? These questions suggest that one can only form a well-founded opinion via the news media. Yet that isn't true. Interestingly, the intellectual fathers of modern democracy (Rousseau, Hume, Locke and Montesquieu) lived in an age before the glut of news – and they still maintained a rich political discourse. This discourse took place partly through books, pamphlets, essays, debating societies and public gatherings, but also in the political salons that sprang up everywhere, most of them organised by women. All of these contributed to a lively political discussion. The great democratic upheavals of the last four hundred years – the American Revolution, the French Revolution, the Revolutions of 1848, the fall of the Soviet Union – did not need current affairs programmes, news websites or feeds.

Let's take another step back in time. In Ancient Greece, two and a half thousand years ago, democracy (albeit a democracy of the elites that excluded women, slaves and men under thirty) functioned without newspapers, TV or the internet. How did people stay informed? They thought, and they debated.

Back to the present day. How should we vote sensibly without the news? My recommendation: look first at what the candidates have achieved and only then at what they've promised. You may have to google this information, and perhaps you'll end up on a news website. This doesn't matter, however, so long as *you* and not the media or machines determine your path through the internet.

When it comes to referendums, the solution is even easier. Step one: consider the proposed suggestion and think for yourself. What are the arguments for and against? If you skip the news for even one day, you'll have enough time to mull over a referendum, and thus become a better democrat. Step two: discuss the issues with two or three friends, trying to get a clear sense of the counterarguments. Personally, only when I can set out the opposing position as well as my own opinion do I feel qualified to discuss the topic and cast my vote.

The news isn't just unimportant to democracy – sometimes it can even be damaging. Nobody doubts that the quality of political discourse in the last thirty years has gone noticeably downhill. This period corresponds precisely with the rising tide of news. Countless private TV and radio stations started broadcasting. Free newspapers flooded the market. Non-stop news channels popped up online. The internet made it possible to disseminate the most irrelevant items of news completely free. Thanks to smartphones, the news found its way into the furthest corner of our private sphere from 2007 onwards: it has been constantly in our hands or tucked in our trouser pockets, sometimes even sliding into bed with us.

The connection between the increasing glut of news and the decreasing quality of political discourse may be a random correlation. But I don't think so. The development is suspiciously reminiscent of a mechanism we recognise from the 'arms race'. Imagine you're at a football game. A few spectators in front of you stand on their tiptoes to get a better view of the field. Now everybody else is forced to stand on their tiptoes. The net gain is zero, and now everybody's calves are cramping up. It's exactly the same with news production and consumption. The louder one outlet screams, the louder all the others have to scream too. The more outrageous one side's arguments, the more outrageous the other side's counterblast has to be. The consequence?

White noise and a polarised society. The news has led to a race to the bottom – and its lowest common denominator is the sensationalist ultra-brief piece of news. You can't stop this race to the bottom all by yourself, nor can you reverse it. But you don't have to take part. Certainly not if you want to be a good democrat.

32

WHAT ABOUT
DEMOCRACY?: PART 2

In the last chapter we saw how you can become a better democrat by abstaining from the news instead of poking your head into the tornado. Let's move on to the second question: if we all stop reading the news, who's going to keep an eye on those in power?

Democracy only works when it's accompanied by a free press that brings the truth to light and depicts situations in all their complexity. This is far harder than reporting the news. What we need, then, are two kinds of journalism. First, we need investigative journalism, which uncovers facts and wrongdoing. Second, we need journalism that describes the bigger picture, providing background information and explanations; this is known as 'explanatory reporting'. Both types are difficult. Both are expensive. Both demand skill on the part of producers and concentration on the part of consumers. Neither are well served by our current news format.

Historically, the most famous example of investigative journalism is Bob Woodward and Carl Bernstein's work for the *Washington Post* on Watergate, the political scandal that cost President Richard Nixon his job. Of course, few investigations are quite that dramatic, especially not those on a local level. This doesn't matter. They're still important. No doubt about it, we do need people to hold those in power to account – globally, regionally and locally. Unfortunately, precious few journalists have the tools to do so. Unlike news journalists, investigative journalists need to invest a good deal of time – sometimes weeks and months – into a piece. This is exactly the opposite of most news articles today, which are often little more than copy-and-paste jobs. Investigative journalists have to know their subject as well as the people they're writing about. They have to leave their comfortable offices and step out into the big wide world. Investigative journalists aren't satisfied with the first story good enough to publish. They dig deeper and get their hands dirty, doing their best to unearth and double-check their facts.

Do these revelatory, occasionally even sensational finds need to be published in the usual bite-size chunks? Absolutely not. It rarely matters whether the revelation comes to light one day, one week or one month sooner or later. What *does* matter is that it's deeply and thoroughly researched. True, Watergate was a piece of investigative journalism that appeared in a daily newspaper, but the articles were very long and thorough – in stark contrast to the usual titbits of news. Bob Woodward and Carl Bernstein could, of course, have published their research in a long magazine article. Or – if these had existed in 1972 – an extensive blog post. Or as a book. Avoiding the news in no way harms the Fourth Estate. Far from it.

You're supporting investigative journalism that is genuinely credible.

The second type of journalism we desperately need is explanatory reporting. This type involves illuminating the background, triggers, driving factors and web of connections behind key events, as well as offering solutions.

Long newspaper and magazine articles, features, documentaries, podcasts and books are all suitable formats for this type of work, which again require very different skills from daily news journalism. At base, explanatory reporters must – like their investigative colleagues – be experts. And one can only be an expert in one area, or two at the most. A journalist who holds forth on ten, twenty, thirty different topics cannot be taken seriously. Their analyses, opinions and 'global explanations' – even if they're expressed with panache – are often worthless.

This book was written in the hope that intelligent journalists will take a step back from the news and switch sides to investigative or explanatory reporting, and that their less talented colleagues will find another job – a boon for society and themselves (after all, it's not like bad journalism is well paid). This means that journalists who take pride in their work will have to develop a circle of competence. They will have to develop expertise in a particular area. And they'll have to be outstanding communicators. It's a dual challenge to which only a few can rise.

These few will demand money in exchange for their knowledge and skills. Who should pay for that? Apart from professional publications, no business model has proven stable enough to support explanatory journalism on a large scale. Yet the more people stop reading the news and start to value quality reporting, the greater the likelihood that one day it will become sustainable. This about-face must be led by consumers. The market will respond accordingly.

33

THE NEWS LUNCH

I have an idea for how we can breathe new life into the public sphere, perhaps even into democracy – without recourse to stultifying news. It goes like this.

Everybody's got to eat. Especially lunch. Sometimes I have lunch by myself in my office. It's quick, and I can listen to an audiobook while I eat. Sometimes I have business lunches. And sometimes I meet up with a friend (yes, even with journalists). No matter who I'm seeing, I've got into the habit of asking the following question: as we're folding our napkins after the meal, what criteria will I use to decide whether it was a successful lunch? The usual answer? If I've learned something true and relevant from my lunch partner (and they from me), something I didn't know before – a fresh perspective that contributes to my understanding of the world – then the lunch was a success.

These lunches are always most valuable and enjoyable when each partner concentrates on *one* thing. This lets us go deep instead of merely scratching the surface. I also learn how my fellow diner thinks about the topic at hand, how they grapple with it, how they draw insight from it – and vice versa. If my lunch partner is a journalist, they will tell me the most important story they're working on. Not two stories. Not three. But one. This is how I learn the nuances of the story, the shades of grey, the generators behind the events, the context and the journalist's attitude (known as meta-information).

After fifteen minutes we swap, and it's my turn. My companion will learn about the one issue – one, not two or three – currently on my mind. It might be a book chapter or a business idea. Again, for fifteen minutes. The rest of the time until the arrival of our final espressos and the bill is filled with other topics or expanding on previous points of discussion. I call this format a 'news lunch'. After every news lunch I walk back to my office feeling invigorated. A meal like that – at least for me – is never a flop.

The idea of the news lunch with its fifteen-minute discussions could easily be adapted and opened up to more people who are hungry for new ideas alongside their fish, meat or veggies. It could be done by renting a room or a restaurant for regular news lunches, then announcing them via an app or a website where people could sign up and pay. They could take place every workday at noon: two brisk lectures of fifteen minutes each and a healthy lunch. A journalist would present his most important current story. The focus would be not on the headline but on the context. The labour that goes into it, the atmosphere, the colour – all must be part of the presentation. The more locally specific the story, the more relevant to most of the participants.

Next, a scholar (or a journalist, if he or she is also an expert) would present a story that's unlikely to appear in the media because it's slow-burning and abstract, offers no opportunity for gaudy images and cannot be told through the lens of a single individual. This second lecture would also last fifteen minutes. After the two talks, there would be a healthy, speedy lunch. The whole thing, meal included, would take sixty minutes, seventy-five at the outside.

What do you think would be discussed during the meal? The two topics, of course. You couldn't find a better opportunity for intelligent lunchtime conversation. As a participant you would also end up meeting new people each time, all of them keen to understand the driving forces behind world events. In short, it would transform an ordinary lunch break into an intellectually, culinarily and socially rich experience. It would even have a touch of the salon, an informal debating institution in the eighteenth century that was very much *en vogue* in Paris and London.

Who should organise these news lunches? It could be restaurants, enterprising individuals or media companies themselves – every participant is a potential subscriber, after all. In big cities there would be room for several competing news lunches. Over time, diners would figure out where the most interesting crowds gathered for lunch and where the most relevant lectures were being held.

The idea might even grow into a movement and spread to several cities. Imagine you're in a new city, you're hungry, and you don't know anybody you can ask to lunch. You could scoff down a hamburger in the corner of some anonymous pub. Or you could do the smart thing and look up where the nearest news lunch is taking place. That way you're guaranteed intelligent conversation, healthy food and exciting people, all within a familiar, reasonably priced structure. Who knows, it might even develop into a kind of worldwide community, albeit without a formal membership. People who've had enough of the empty calories in conventional media and are starved of a deeper understanding of the world.

'Avoid trifling conversation,' advised Benjamin Franklin in one of his thirteen maxims. This is especially true at mealtimes: a good lunch should be nourishing in all respects.

34

THE FUTURE OF THE NEWS

Where are we headed? As I see it, there are four main trends.

Trend number one: the torrent of news increases exponentially. The more people living on the planet, the more will happen – records, inventions, atrocities, miracles, inconceivable things. A town of ten thousand people will generate far less newsworthy material than a society of ten billion. The number of possible interactions *between* people and therefore the number of potential news stories increases exponentially. In addition, the cost of producing and publishing the news is sinking towards zero. The net result will be an exponential rather than linear increase in the output of news. The relevance to an individual person's life will remain virtually nil, however, even as the levels of white noise are exploding.

Trend number two: the news is all around us, all the time. In the old days, people read, watched and listened to the news at particular times and particular places. There were windows of time with the news and windows of time without the news. There were places with the news and places without the news. Today, the news has infiltrated many areas of our public and private lives at all hours of the day. This trend looks set to continue. What's driving this trend is – as is so often the case – the unholy alliance between news and advertising. This means that the interests of news producers and news consumers are not precisely aligned. The news pursues us at work, and it pursues us onto the toilet and into the bedroom via our smartphones. There are bathroom mirrors that will play you the news as you're brushing your teeth in the morning. Climb into any New York taxi and instantly you're awash in it. Maybe soon there will be free designer sunglasses that regularly feed us a mixture of news and advertising in exchange for the privilege of wearing them. The news is omnipresent. If you want to escape it, you have to take radical action.

Trend number three: algorithms are getting better all the time at understanding us. Wherever you leave digital traces (on Google, Facebook, Amazon, Apple, your hosting provider and news websites), programs are busily drawing up an increasingly precise picture of your personality. Many of these algorithms already know you better than you could describe yourself – your preferences, your political leanings, your consumer behaviour, your career, your leisure pursuits, your relationships, your daily routine, your desires, worries and needs. These algorithms know how to hook you emotionally. They know your emotional buttons better than your partner, so they deliberately lure you with the articles, images and videos to which you are most receptive. Unfortunately, they're not doing it out of the goodness of their hearts. Behind these cool, calculating machines are the owners of the corporations (the shareholders), who want to see money – your money. When it comes down to it, they're always trying to sell you something – advertising, products, political opinions, world views. Of course, this was also the case with newspapers. They, too, are financed largely through advertising. They, too, use news as bait, trying to draw your attention to the adverts. But printed newspapers knew nothing about you, so their impact was minimal. Today's algorithms use morsels of news ('click-bait', to use the jargon) in an altogether more targeted way. The upshot? It's getting increasingly difficult to distance ourselves from the stream of news. Imagine if cigarettes, alcohol and cocaine were not only free but actually offered to you on all sides, round the clock, by invisible hands. There's no doubt most of us would be hooked. This is precisely what's happening with the news today. The inhibition threshold for a news addiction isn't just low, it isn't just zero – it's actually negative. It takes far more discipline to avoid the news than to procure it.

Trend number four: the news is drifting further and further from the truth. Not only are algorithms getting better at calculating what will grab your attention, they are also getting more creative all the time. Even today, programs are able to use artificial intelligence to create text, images and videos without human aid. Within the next few years, these artificially generated products will be indistinguishable from the real thing. Fake news will become more appealing than the actual news. It's perfectly logical. After all, they're designed purely and simply to attract attention. They no longer need to worry about reality. Who, you may be wondering, would be interested in disseminating fake news? It's simple: any organisation that wants to hold your attention captive for as long as possible so that it can feed you adverts and drain you of data. Or any organisation that wants to manipulate your opinions, especially political ones. Fake news has always been with us – pamphlets at the end of the Middle Ages, propaganda during wartime. The crucial difference is that, in the future, these fakes will no longer be actively created by human beings. Whereas in the old days there were identifiable people behind the lies – people who had to answer to their consciences – soon there will only be computer programs.

The danger is growing all the time that the news will turn our brains to mush. Fresh waves of news are breaking over us constantly, each one bigger than the last. Get out while you still have the strength. Time is running out.

35

HOW IT FEELS

On 26 January 1649, Charles I, King of England, Scotland and Ireland, was condemned to death. His attempt to do away with parliament had precipitated a civil war – a war he lost. Like all kings of that era, Charles thought he had a divine right to rule, and a not-insignificant part of the population believed him. It was the first time in the history of Europe that a king had ever been executed. Uncertainty rippled across the continent. Was this even permissible? What might the consequences be? Would God plunge the world into chaos?

On 30 January 1649, at two o'clock precisely, in front of thousands of spectators, the king climbed the scaffold and placed his head on the block. After a short prayer he signalled to the executioner that he was ready to die. One clean swing of the axe was enough, and his head rolled off. A groan swept through the crowd. A few dipped their handkerchiefs in the pooling blood.

The next day, 31 January, life went on. The Thames kept flowing, the birds twittered as though nothing had happened, the sun rose at the expected time, the cows produced milk, the bakers baked bread, children were born, birthdays were celebrated and the world kept turning even without the king.

I've observed a certain reverence for the news similar to that once reserved for kings. Many people's initial reaction to the idea of giving up the news is to ask, *Is that even allowed?* As though all sense of meaning would disappear in a puff of smoke and society would collapse, solely because we decided to stop reading the newspaper. Sounds ridiculous, but for many people living without the news is truly unimaginable, the way it was unimaginable living without a king 350 years ago. Of course, the media pulls out all the stops to maintain its aura of relevance. On TV they do it with impressive trailers cutting swiftly from plane crashes to rockets taking off to presidents to the spinning planet – all set to bombastic music. It's a spectacle designed to say: this is about everything. And yet, it's about nothing at all.

For hundreds of years, the king sat unquestioned on his throne – then he was beheaded, and suddenly everybody realised: *we don't need one*. It's exactly the same with the news. At first, a total ban seems daring, immoral, egotistical, heretical. Yet our grandchildren will look back at today's news junkies and shake their heads.

When you first stop reading the news, you'll probably be gripped by the subtle sense that you're doing something radical. It was like that for me, anyway. Like I'd done something improper. Like staying informed about everything was the duty of any decent citizen. At first I wasn't sure whether it was going to be a short-lived experiment, some indulgent folly I would jettison again after a week or two.

Back then my arguments were still embryonic. I kept my experiment under wraps, discussing it with no one. If the conversation turned to current events, I tried to act as though I'd read the news and simply not given it much thought. I smiled along when other people laughed about something they'd seen on the evening TV news programme, *Tagesschau*. I assumed a thoughtful expression when someone mentioned a natural disaster on the other side of the world, letting it seem as though *of course* the disaster hadn't escaped my notice, but that I'd already processed it mentally – and thus was incapable of spontaneous emotional outbursts. Basically, I faked my way through as best I could. I quailed at meeting people I didn't know, because those meetings always involved small talk, and small talk – after we'd exhausted the weather – always turned to current affairs. I found it embarrassing to discuss my experiment.

In time, however, I grew more confident that I was on the right track. My arguments became sharper, my attitude clearer, time more elastic, my decision-making better, my peace of mind more profound. You, too, will experience the same thing in your own body. You, dear reader, are now fully equipped with an array of arguments against consuming the news. All you have to do is implement them.

Are you afraid that living news-free will make you seem boring at parties? Don't worry. You may not know that the president just wrote an annoying tweet, but you understand the world better now and you can share that understanding with your friends. Don't feel shy about discussing your new lifestyle. People will be fascinated to listen. And if the conversation does judder to a halt, there's no better way to jump-start it than with the following question: 'So, what do you think are the most important headlines this week?' You'll see – most people will *love* explaining things to you. And they'll love you for giving them an opportunity to share their immense but pointless store of trivia. Accept it with a knowing smile.

ACKNOWLEDGEMENTS

Thanks are due to Koni Gebistorf, who copy-edited this text with a sure hand and gave it the necessary polish.

I don't know a more professional non-fiction editor than Martin Janik from Piper Verlag. He worked on my previous books – *The Art of Thinking Clearly* and *The Art of the Good Life* – and I'm delighted he worked on this as well.

Nassim Taleb was the first person to bring news-induced cognitive errors to my attention. I'm grateful to him for many of these insights – though by now I'm no longer sure exactly which ones. I wrote the original essay in English. René Scheu, then editor of the *Schweizer Monat* and currently features editor at the *Neue Zürcher Zeitung*, translated it into German in 2011 and printed it in the *Schweizer Monat*.

This book would not exist without the countless conversations, emails and letters I've exchanged over the years on the topic of the news. In no particular order, I want to thank the following people for their valuable ideas: Thomas and Esther Schenk, Manfred Lütz, Kipper Blakeley, Valerie von der Malsburg, Peter Bevelin, Matt Ridley, Michael Hengartner, Martin Vetterli, Guy Spier, Tom Ladner, Alex

Wassmer, Schoscho Rufener, Marc Walder, Ksenija Sidorova, Georges Kern, Avi Avital, Uli Sigg, Numa and Corinne Bischof Ullmann, Rolf and Elisabeth Jenni, Barbara and Riccardo Ciarpaglini, Holger Ried, Erich Bagus, Wolfgang Schürer, Anja Hergenröther, Ewald Ried, Marcel Rohner, Nils Hagander, Stefan Brupbacher, Lorenz Furrer, Nicole Loeb, Andreas Meyer, Thomas Wellauer, Urs Wietlisbach, Walter Thurnherr, Norbert Riedel, Raffaello D'Andrea, Daniel and Adrienne Surbek, Myriam and François Geelhaar, Lou Marinoff, Tom Wujec, Urs Baumann, Pascal Forster, Martin Spieler, Georg Diez, Angela and Axel Keuneke, Daniel Dennett, Ruedi Matter, Christoph Tonini, Simon Bärtschi, Marc Werner, Christian Dorer, Gieri Cavelty, Jean-Rémy von Matt, my parents Ruth and Ueli, and the sadly deceased Franz Kaufmann.

The biggest thanks of all is due to my wife. She stopped reading the news long before I did – even before I was lucky enough to meet her. She is a sparkling fount of ideas. And she is my first editor. Her merciless red pen is a gift to you, dear reader.

148

THE DOBELLI DISCLAIMER

The theses in this book – and this is true of all my non-fiction writing – reflect the clearest and truest view of things I was able to achieve by the date of publication. I reserve the right to revise my theses at any time. I might even allow myself the pleasure of self-contradiction. The only reason why I would revise my theses or contradict myself is to get closer to the truth. Never for personal advantage.

APPENDIX

I have restricted myself to the most important technical references and recommended reading here, though not for every chapter. Obviously my inspiration and insights come from all over and cannot always be attributed to one specific source.

You Could Have Heard a Pin Drop
In spring 2011 I published an initial version of the article on my website. None of my other articles has precipitated more responses (either in protest or agreement).

The short version of this article was published in the *Guardian*: 'News is bad for you – and giving up reading it will make you happier' (www.theguardian.com/media/ 2013/apr/12/news-is-bad-rolf-dobelli).

From 1995 to 2015 Alan Rusbridger was editor-in-chief of the *Guardian*, one of the oldest daily newspapers in the UK. During his tenure he witnessed the politically delicate coverage of the WikiLeaks documents. In 2018 he published the brilliant book *Breaking News: The Remaking of Journalism and Why It Matters Now* (Canongate Books, Edinburgh, 2018) – a critique of news journalism.

3. News is to the Mind What Sugar is to the Body
If you'd like to learn more about the history of the news, I'd recommend the following books: Andrew Pettegree, *The Invention of News: How the World Came to Know About Itself* (Yale University Press, Cambridge, Mass., 2014) and Mitchell Stephens, *A History of News* (Harcourt Brace College Publishers, London, 1997).

5. The Thirty-Day Plan
For more on escaping the everyday to think, see: www.theladders.com/career-advice/how-to-take-a-think-week-or-day-like-bill-gates and Rebecca Muller: 'Bill Gates Spends Two Weeks Alone In the Forest Each Year. Here's Why.' in, *Thrive Global*, 23 July 2018 (www.thriveglobal. com/stories/bill-gates-think-week/).

The most significant invention of 1993 was the first graphical internet browser, Mosaic. Version 1.0, for Microsoft Windows, first saw the light of day on 11 November (www.ncsa.illinois.edu/enabling/mosaic).

9. News is Outside Your Circle of Competence
Elena Holodny: 'Isaac Newton was a genius, but even he lost millions in the stock market' in *Business Insider*, 10 November 2017 (www.businessinsider.com/isaac-newton-lost-a-fortune-on-englands-hottest-stock-2016-1).

10. News Gets Risk Assessment All Wrong
The car driving over the bridge example is drawn from Nassim Nicholas Taleb (personal correspondence).

There's a great example of inaccurate risk assessment in Jodie Jackson's book *You Are What You Read: Why Changing Your Media Diet Can Change the World* (Unbound Publishing, London, 2019), p.61. (The original study is here: www.ons.gov.uk/peoplepopulationandcommunity/crimeandjustice/articles/publicperceptionsof-crimeinenglandandwales/yearendingmarch2016)

11. News is a Waste of Time
See the Pew Research Center data for more information.

12. News Obscures the Big Picture
On peering into the engine room see Gavin Schmidt, *The Disconnect Between News and Understanding*, NASA's Goddard Institute for Space Studies, in John Brockman (ed.), *What Should We Be Worried About?* Harper Perennial, New York, 2014.

See also, www.er.ethz.ch/teaching/Seven_ Sins_fund_ Management.pdf. See also Max Frisch, *Montauk*, (Suhrkamp Verlag, Frankfurt am Main, 1975), p.36.

13. News is Toxic to Your Body
For the adrenaline-cortisol stress reaction, see Robert M. Sapolsky, Lewis C. Krey and Bruce S. McEwen, 'The neuro-endocrinology of stress and aging: the glucocorticoid cascade hypothesis', in *Endocrine Reviews*, 7, 1986, pp.284–301.

For adverse impact of the news on our health see, www.time.com/5125894/is-reading-news-bad-for-you/. The original research paper: Wendy M. Johnston and Graham

Davey, 'The psychological impact of negative TV news bulletins: The catastrophizing of personal worries' in *British Journal of Psychology*, 88, 1997 (Pt 1), pp.85–91.

See also Dagmar Unz, Frank Schwab and Peter Winterhoff-Spurk, 'TV News – The Daily Horror?: Emotional Effects of Violent Television News.' in *Journal of Media Psychology: Theories, Methods, and Applications*, 20, 2008, pp.141–155.

A study on the terrorist attacks of 11 September 2001 shows that media consumption (TV hours on the subject of the World Trade Center attacks) was linked to post-traumatic stress. E. B. Blanchard, E. Kuhn, D. L. Rowell, E. J. Hickling, D. Wittrock, R. L. Rogers, M. R. Johnson and D. C. Steckler, 'Studies of the vicarious traumatization of college students by the September 11th attacks: Effects of proximity, exposure and connectedness.' (www.ncbi.nlm.nih.gov/pubmed/14975780) in *Behaviour Research and Therapy*, Volume 42, Issue 2, February 2004, pp.191–205.

15. News Reinforces Hindsight Bias

On 'because of X', Nassim Nicholas Taleb has written about the journalistic urge to find the one reason for something in *The Black Swan: The Impact of the Highly Improbable* (Penguin Books, London, 2008). Also see, Nassim Nicholas Taleb, *Antifragile: Things that Gain from Disorder* (Penguin Books, London, 2012). See also Roy F. Baumeister, *The Cultural Animal: Human Nature, Meaning, and Social Life* (Oxford University Press, Oxford, 2005), p.206 ff.

16. News Reinforces Availability Bias

On the prevention of 9/11 by installing locks on cockpit doors, see Taleb, *The Black Swan*, p.xxiii–xxiv. See also Matt Ridley, 'Why Is It So Cool to Be Gloomy?' in the *Wall Street Journal*, 16 November 2018.

On the confusion between 'preventative' and 'non-existent', see Jackson, *You Are What You Read*. This is a superb manifesto for constructive journalism. Constructive journalism aims to also report on preventative success stories, thus making them 'existent' in the reader's mind.

17. News Keeps the Opinion Volcano Bubbling

See Marcus Aurelius, *Meditations*, Book 6, paragraph 52, translated by Martin Hammond (Penguin Books, London, 2006).

18. News Inhibits Thought

See Nicholas Carr, 'The Web Shatters Focus, Rewires Brains' in *Wired*, May 2010.

19. News Rewires Our Brains

See Carr, 'The Web Shatters Focus, Rewires Brains' in *Wired*, May 2010.

On London cabbies see Eleanor A. Maguire, Katherine Woollett and Hugo J. Spiers, 'London Taxi Drivers and Bus Drivers: A Structural MRI and Neuropsychological Analysis', *Hippocampus*, 16, 2006, pp.1091–1101. On the new geometric drawings, see the Rey–Osterrieth Complex Figure test.

See also Kep-Kee Loh and Ryota Kanai, 'Higher Media

Multi-Tasking Activity Is Associated with Smaller Gray-Matter Density in the Anterior Cingulate Cortex' in *PLOS One*, 2014.

20. News Produces Fake Fame

On Donald Henderson see Alison F. Takemura, 'Epidemiologist Who Helped Eradicate Smallpox Dies' in *The Scientist*, 22 August 2016 (www.the-scientist.com/the-nutshell/epidemiologist-who-helped-eradicate-smallpox-dies-32993).

21. News Makes Us Smaller Than We Really Are

See Michael Marmot, *Social Determinants of Health*, WORLD.MINDS video, 2014 (www.youtube.com/watch?v=h-2bf205upQ).

22. News Makes Us Passive

On the rat experiment see Steven Maier, 'Stress, coping, resilience and the prefrontal cortex' (www.youtube.com/watch?v=0EhbTSWZbMg).

Epictetus never published anything. These notes were recorded by Arrian, one of his pupils.

23. News is Invented by Journalists

On the employment statistics see CareerCast survey of jobs, 2015 (www.careercast.com/jobs-rated/jobs-rated-report-2015-ranking-top-200-jobs?page=9), and CareerCast survey of jobs, 2018 (www.careercast.com/jobs-rated/2018-jobs-rated-report?page=10). The CareerCast criteria are here: www.careercast.com/jobs-rated/2018-methodology.

On 'the race to the bottom', see Jaron Lanier, *Ten*

Arguments For Deleting Your Social Media Accounts Right Now (Henry Holt, New York, 2018), p.33.

On 'slow journalism', see Jennifer Rauch, *Slow Media: Why "Slow" is Satisfying, Sustainable, and Smart* (Oxford University Press, New York, 2018) and Peter Laufer, *Slow News: A Manifesto for the Critical News Consumer* (Oregon State University Press, Corvallis, 2014). Again I'd refer you to Jackson's convincing manifesto on 'constructive journalism', *You Are What You Read*. A book that offers a similar critique of the news media but does not use those labels is Rusbridger's *Breaking News*.

24. News is Manipulative

See Pettegree, *The Invention of News*, p. 2. Also Clay A. Johnson, *The Information Diet: A Case for Conscious Consumption* (O'Reilly Media, Beijing, 2015), p.40.

On the size of the global PR industry see The Holmes Report, which puts the size of the international PR industry at fifteen billion dollars (www.holmesreport.com/long-reads/article/global-pr-industry-now-worth-$15bn-as-growth-rebounds-to-7-in-2016). One PR industry estimate limited to Great Britain puts the figure at roughly the same size (www.prca.org.uk/insights/about-pr-industry/value-and-size-pr-industry). This would mean the global PR industry was much bigger. This statistic assumes a global turnover of twenty billion dollars (www.statista.com/topics/3521/public-relations/).

On fake content see Max Read: 'How Much of the Internet Is Fake? Turns Out, a Lot of It, Actually.' in *New York Magazine*, 26 December 2018.

See also Jill Lepore, 'Does Journalism Have a Future?' in the *New Yorker*, 28 January 2019. (www.newyorker.com/magazine/2019/01/28/does-journalism-have-a-future).

See Yuval Noah Harari for insight into free news in his books and in the *Guardian*, 5 August 2018, 'Humans are a post-truth species' (www.theguardian.com/culture/2018/aug/05/yuval-noah-harari-extract-fake-news-sapiens-homo-deus).

For more on manipulation and propaganda, see Pettegree, *The Invention of News*, pp.6–7. And about historical precedents of Russian news interference, p.35.

25. News Kills Creativity
On the difficulty of forming one's own thoughts see William Deresiewicz, 'Solitude and Leadership. If you want others to follow, learn to be alone with your thoughts.' in *The American Scholar*, 1 March 2010 (www.theamerican scholar.org/solitude-and-leadership/#.XDcLLC1oTOQ).

See also Max Frisch's diaries, *Tagebuch 1966–1971* (Suhrkamp Verlag, Frankfurt and Main, 1972), p.314.

26. News Encourages Crap: Sturgeon's Law
For more on Ernest Hemingway see Robert Manning, 'Hemingway in Cuba' in *The Atlantic*, August 1965 (www.theatlantic.com/magazine/archive/1965/08/hemingway-in-cuba/399059/).

28. News Encourages Terrorism
For more on terrorism see the writings of Martha Crenshaw, Professor of Political Science at Stanford University, and

useful statistics, both on ourworldindata.org. For global death toll of different causes of death see Oxfam research (oxfamblogs.org/fp2p/what-if-we-allocated-aid-based-on-how-much-damage-something-does-and-whether-we-know-how-to-fix-it/). See also Yuval Noah Harari, *21 Lessons for the 21st Century* (Jonathan Cape, London, 2018), p.161.

29. News Destroys Our Peace of Mind

For ideas from Seneca see Jack Reeves, 'Seneca's Smartphone: Stoic Principles for Managing Digital Distraction' (www.modernstoicism.com/senecas-smartphone-stoic-principles-for-managing-digital-distraction-by-jack-reeves/#comment-26015).

For a wonderful satire on the agitation generated by the news, see Colin Nissan, 'Bad News' in the *New Yorker*, 23 July 2018 (www.newyorker.com/magazine/2018/07/23/bad-news).

30. Not Convinced?

On reading old newspapers, see Nassim Nicholas Taleb, *The Bed of Procrustes* (Random House, New York, 2010), p.28.

32. What About Democracy?: Part 2

For more on Watergate see www.washingtonpost.com/wpsrv/national/longterm/watergate/articles/101072–1.htm

On the pressure on news journalists, see Johnson, *The Information Diet*, p.35. See also Lanier, *Ten Arguments For Deleting Your Social Media Accounts Right Now*, p.68.

34. The Future of the News

On Trend Three, the algorithm, see Lanier, *Ten Arguments For Deleting Your Social Media Accounts Right Now*, p.11.

On Trend Four, fake news written by AI programs, see Will Knight, 'An AI that writes convincing prose risks mass-producing fake news' in *MIT Technology Review*, 14 February 2019 (www.technologyreview.com/s/612960/an-ai-tool-auto-generates-fake-news-bogus-tweets-and-plenty-of-gibberish/).

Join a literary community of
like-minded readers who seek out
the best in contemporary writing.

From the thousands of submissions Sceptre
receives each year, our editors select the books
we consider to be outstanding.

We look for distinctive voices, thought-provoking
themes, original ideas, absorbing narratives and
writing of prize-winning quality.

If you want to be the first to hear about our
new discoveries, and would like the chance to
receive advance reading copies of our books
before they are published, visit

www.sceptrebooks.co.uk

 Follow @sceptrebooks

 'Like' SceptreBooks

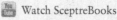 Watch SceptreBooks